When Children Read

BY

CHARLES F. REASONER

Professor
New York University

A YEARLING BOOK

Acknowledgments

My special appreciation is extended to the following extraordinary teachers with whom I've had the privilege of working and from whom came ideas and suggestions—some of which I've modified and included in this book:

Jodi Cotler	*Arlene Pillar*
Ann Dorfman	*Jack Rubel*
Judith Engel	*Mary Schoolman*
Marilyn Griffin	*Reevan Tucker*
Rosanne Kaufman	*Sharon Willison*

Published by
Dell Publishing Co., Inc.
1 Dag Hammarskjold Plaza
New York, New York 10017

Yearling ® TM 913705, Dell Publishing Co., Inc.
ISBN: 0-440-49464-8
Printed in the United States of America

Third Dell printing—June 1981

MPC

2218783

For K.W.

CONTENTS

Page references to Yearling Books are for large-format editions only.

FOREWORD

POOH LOOKED AT HIS TWO PAWS. HE KNEW
THAT ONE OF THEM WAS THE RIGHT, AND
HE KNEW THAT WHEN YOU HAD DECIDED
WHICH ONE OF THEM WAS THE RIGHT,
THEN THE OTHER WAS THE LEFT, BUT HE
NEVER COULD REMEMBER HOW TO BEGIN.

The House at Pooh Corner
by A. A. Milne, New York: Dell Yearling, 1975

Just as Pooh found out that there is more to *knowing* than
simply *knowing about* left and right, today's teachers have
learned that *knowing about* children is not exactly the same
thing as *knowing* children; that *knowing about* books for children is quite different from *knowing* them.

It is not always easy for teachers to decide where to begin
—even though they know where they want to go. It might be
that the place for one to begin is at the point where *knowing
about* and *knowing* converge so that the excitement and satisfaction in teaching result from discovering one's own beginnings.
When Children Read is a teacher's guide which attempts to
point out ways, but not to prescribe; to provide alternatives,
but not panaceas; to free teachers to be inventive and innovative instead of restraining them with fixed materials and methods
for using them. It is not for the teacher who needs to be told
where to begin.

This book—like *Releasing Children to Literature* and
Where the Readers Are—is for the *creative* teacher, the one who
works in such ways as to allow children to become more different
rather than more alike. This book—like its predecessors—is for

9

the *different* teacher, the one who has grown beyond those traditional, anxious attempts to keep children's comprehension uniform and toward the greater satisfactions to be gained from uncovering the individual child's responses to literature encounters. This book—like the previous two—is for the innovative teacher, the one who is able to see relationships between the practical activities presented and the ways they may need to be varied and adapted to the individual differences of the learners in a particular classroom situation.

It is not always easy for me to understand why some teachers talk about searching for ways to coax and "motivate" children to *want to read*—as if reading were a bitter pill to be swallowed. A classroom library of fine paperback books provides the ideal setting for books and children to attract one another—an open invitation for them to get together. When a child has many opportunities to satisfy his/her reading desires by choosing from a variety of titles, books will not be distasteful. They will not be inappropriate. They will not need outside stimuli. Children WANT to read. Children DO read. And, children WILL READ without coercion or extrinsic rewards when the reading fare is *right:* the right material, for the right child, at the right time.

However, in this day of stating educational objectives in behavioral terms, many teachers are concerned about what to do *when children read* without manipulating children's responses toward predetermined answers. Also, there is no less concern about the disenchantment so many teachers have found in "doing nothing" once they have made many fine books easily accessible to young readers. They want *feedback* because such information is so vital to teachers who strive to *know* children.

While most of this book deals specifically with the practical, "classroom-tested" activities for each of the twenty titles, on the few introductory pages which follow, I continue the discussions which I started with teachers in *Releasing Children to Literature* and *Where the Readers Are*. They are my responses to some of the many "classroom-management" questions which many teachers have asked. They are representative of some of the obstacles which teachers tell me are most likely to thwart their attempts to work with individual children as they choose the books they want to read as well as when and how they elect to react to what they have read.

"It's a poor sort of memory that only works backwards," insisted the White Queen in Lewis Carroll's *Through the Looking-glass*.

Remembering how to begin may be a kind of looking backward that holds little promise for teachers who want to provide exciting options for children *when they read*. The time has come to look ahead.

Charles F. Reasoner
Manhasset, New York
January 1975

AN IMPORTANT WORD TO TEACHERS ABOUT INDIVIDUALIZATION AND LITERATURE

There probably is no other point where experts in the teaching of reading come close to unanimous agreement than that which recognizes that each child's needs be treated individually as well as the fact that what may work with one student may not work for another.

While there is nothing really new about arranging classroom conditions so that it is possible to work more on a one-to-one basis with learners, many teachers are finding the results of their attempts to "individualize" falling far short of the high hopes they had expected. Perhaps one of the reasons for this is the erroneous notion that individualization is little more than turning students loose to work with kits, packets, or in learning centers. *While INDEPENDENT STUDY is an important facet of individualization, it is not an accurate synonym.*

Or, perhaps the results have been disappointing because of the oversimplified notion that allowing children choices justifies the existence of some of the *laissez-faire* conditions in some classrooms where there are few, if any, expectations and/or requirements for pupils and little or no planning and structure of the school day. Choices *without manipulation* are essential to the kind of classroom organization which recognizes the *learner* as the "individualizer" of his/her curriculum but disallows the idea that children are free to read or not read, write or not write, select or not select to do math, engage or not engage in science, social studies, and so forth.

Or, perhaps some teachers have found their attempts to individualize not as satisfying as they had expected because of uncritical acceptance of some of the *myths* which have been spawned by the many enthusiastic proponents of "The Individualized Approach" whereby precise "How-to Methods" are spelled out uniformly for *all* teachers—ignoring the fact that teachers, too, are individuals! For example, the *myth* that the teacher must see each child in a "conference" each day. Or, the *myth* that the conference time is spent chit-chatting about the child's comprehension (something that consumes a great deal of classroom time). Or, the *myth* that there is such a thing as an "average learner"; that there actually exists such a person as a "fourth-grade-pupil." Or, the *myth* that required textbooks and/or a required curriculum to be covered are insurmountable hurdles and are, therefore, incompatible with individualized paradigms. Or, the *myth* that claims that evaluation and grading are impossible (and therefore irrelevant) when one works individually with children.

Whatever the reasons, the fact remains that while most teachers believe in individualization, very few are convinced that, practically, it's a type of organizational plan which can be implemented in today's classroom. Most of these problems, along with numerous others, actually are "classroom-management" problems rather than difficulties that can be solved by special materials, innovative methods, and the like. It also is true that probably more harm than good has come from the rather popular practice of isolating separate elementary-school subjects "for individualizing," such as: "Individualized Reading," or "Individualized Math," or "Individualized Spelling," and so forth. Actually, individualization is more of a *state of mind—a commitment*—than anything else. It is a view of teaching whereby teachers believe that *all* children have the right to succeed—not fail; that successful classroom experiences cause children to become more different rather than more alike by trying to get them to (or keeping them all on) "level." Then, too, some teachers have become confused by many of the "new" concepts which have arrived on the educational scene, such as "Open Classrooms," or "Learning Centers," or "Non-Graded-ness,"

13

all of which have been acclaimed as systems relying heavily on "the individualized approach."

The temptation to respond to these many facets of individualization must give way to limiting the discussion to the problems of using literature in those classroom settings when—*individually*—children read.

When children read literature, individuals will need more time to make selections: to browse, sample, return books, and choose others. Individuals will need to have options to select *the time* when they are in their most appropriate and receptive moods for reading. Time choices include, for example, allowing an individual all morning, all afternoon, or even the best part of a whole day to finish a book when—on one of those rare occasions—one discovers a book he/she just can't put down.

When children read literature, individuals need to be permitted the choice to select *where* they read best—in school, at home, on the playground, in the hall, a ball park, at a desk, on the floor, alone, in a group. Some individuals derive great pleasure in and satisfaction from reading to a friend—or a group of friends. Opportunities for children to gather for literature readings (with and *without* the teacher) are important needs which must be provided for in classrooms where children read.

When children read literature, elementary-school teachers have discovered that they can learn about what individual students comprehend from their literature encounters by providing them with a variety of choices from which they may choose (like those included in each of the sections called "Helping Children to Reveal Their Comprehension") in order to share their interpretations of book ideas with the teacher, and that the time spent in teacher-pupil conferences is best utilized by *diagnosing* individual reading-skill needs and then *teaching* the child the skill he/she needs without regard to age/grade placement. Any printed material may be used for these *diagnostic/teaching* skill sessions including textbooks, *TV Guide,* bubble-gum trading cards, or comic books—and, of course, fine trade books as well.

When children read literature, care must be taken to avoid public display of what children read—whether creative charts or simple bulletin board posters. Almost always this leads to nurturing undesirable competitive reading for *quantity* wherein children choose "easy" books, or report reading books which they haven't read, or listing books they've read in previous years, and so forth. Records need to be kept by pupils and teachers alike. However, the records children keep need to be brief and simple if they are to be valuable not only as records but as diagnostic tools as well. Children soon become weary and suspicious of the kinds of *forms* which ask them to comment "briefly" about (1) the exciting parts, (2) the funniest incident, (3) my favorite character in the story, (4) why I would recommend this book to my friend, (5) how I would change the ending, and so on. Perhaps this is how some teachers feel they need to discern a child's comprehension as well as to discover whether or not he/she has been truthful in reading what he/she said he/she read—especially if a child's book selection is unfamiliar to the teacher. On the other hand, children have responded quite enthusiastically—and with honesty—when teachers have invited them to keep track of *everything* they read, *both in and out of school* (which they don't object revealing to the teacher) on a rather simple record form calling only for information as: (1) name of the book or material, (2) author/source, (3) date when reading began, (4) date when reading stopped—or book (or other material) was completed. From these records teachers may compile their own logs of what children read.

When children read literature, it is reasonable for teachers to have minimum expectations for individual students. Such expectations might include the number of books to be read over a given marking period (although I have never found this to be necessary at all) as well as which two or three of the many books a child reads during this period he/she desires to select for purposes of sharing comprehension responses with the teacher. Reading goals, however, are negated when teachers attempt to wean children's choices away from certain literature categories such as talking-animal stories, or mysteries, or science fiction in order to make them "well-rounded" readers—as if to protect them from their own "lusts." It is also somewhat less than honest to provide choices for children's reading and comprehension responses and then attempt to guide them away from (or even disallow) certain choices which some individuals may become hooked on and thus be inclined to choose to do over and over again.

When children read literature, evaluation of individual students can be managed accurately and fairly if teachers keep *all evidence* on file in the classroom—resisting the traditional practice of sending papers home. At the end of each marking period, professional accountability is possible by examining the reading records discussed above as well as the comprehension-revealing activities/experiences each child completes, dates, and files in a folder of his/her own. This avoids the dehumanizing practice of comparing one learner with another or with some artificial norm or standard and will do more to reverse the current objections to "individualization" than anything else. Part of the teaching responsibility is to assess, evaluate, and (in most instances) grade. The professional responsibility is to do this as efficiently and as accurately as possible. All the data need to be examined and studied to assess individual growth; therefore the individual's progress is compared only with his/her past performances or his/her "learning-departure" point and not with the abilities and performances of others.

"WHAT IS REAL?" ASKED THE RABBIT ONE DAY. "DOES IT MEAN HAVING THINGS THAT BUZZ INSIDE YOU AND A STICK-OUT HANDLE?"

"REAL ISN'T HOW YOU ARE MADE," SAID THE SKIN HORSE, "IT'S A THING THAT HAPPENS TO YOU. WHEN A CHILD LOVES YOU FOR A LONG, LONG TIME, NOT JUST TO PLAY WITH, BUT REALLY LOVES YOU, THEN YOU BECOME REAL."

The Velveteen Rabbit
by Margery Williams, New York: Avon Books, 1975.

Books are not kept alive by writers. Authors merely set their ideas free between the covers of books. It is the reader who gives them their chance at greatness. When a book reaches the stature of a classic, it is because it has been loved many times over by children throughout their lives. It becomes *real* because it lives with them as well as through them.

Since a person's experiences grow and change as he/she lives, good books possess the quality of inviting numerous rereadings. As a child grows older, he/she has more to bring to subsequent readings of familiar titles because he/she has accumulated more and different experiences. As a result, such a reader takes more away from his/her second or third contact with a good book because he/she has given more to it.

A good book—a work of literary excellence—has the quality of speaking to its readers between the lines. It is this quality that makes a book *real*. It is this quality that makes writers of good books seem to say more than they actually put down on paper. In between the lines are innuendos, imagery, signs, and signals for perceptive readers to pick up, flash against a background of unique personal experiencing, and create *with writers* arresting moments of life which not only spring from, but transcend, characters and plot and go on living with them for a long, long time.

A book becomes *real* when a child has opportunities to live with it for a while; when he/she is able to have it with him/her, take it to heart, to know and love it. Living with fine books becomes a personal experience for young children not unlike other experiences they desire, seek out, find, and remember—*when children read*.

LITERATURE GUIDES FOR YEARLING BOOKS

BEN AND ME

Written and Illustrated by

ROBERT LAWSON

I. THE STORY

This is the famous book in which Amos immodestly reveals that
he, Dr. Franklin's closest friend and adviser, was largely responsible for the great man's inventions, discoveries, and successes—especially at the French court.

II. PREREADING DISCUSSION QUESTIONS

*The questions which follow are illustrative of the kinds which
teachers can prepare for the purpose of releasing children to
reveal how* they feel *about some of the larger ideas and bigger
meanings contained in the book* before it is read by the children.

About Animal Advisers
1. What can you tell about different animals who seem to
   give humans "advice" or warnings?

2. For many years, scientists have been using different animals in experiments, from medicine to space flights. What animal experiment do you know about? Why was the particular animal used? What information did the scientists learn?
3. What game or experiment have you created with a pet?
4. What "work" do animals do that would be difficult, if not impossible, for humans to do?

About Making Mistakes

5. What mistakes can you think of that are *valuable?*
6. What kinds of mistakes are you most afraid of making?
7. What kinds of mistakes do you think are the most embarrassing?
8. Why do you think people try to keep from making mistakes?
9. What example can you give that clearly shows what a goof means? A *faux pas?* An accident?

About Agreements and Disagreements

10. What feelings do you have about someone you like and trust when he/she breaks a promise to you?
11. Most people consider written contracts, agreements, and promises legal, honorable, unbreakable understandings. What written understandings do you have down on paper? What could happen to cause you to want to break such an agreement?
12. What reasons can you give that explain why people say to one another: *"Be sure to put it down in black and white!"?*
13. What kind of person can you imagine who would take *the credit* for ideas or work which someone else has done? What could cause someone to let another take credit for things he/she has done? How many examples can you give of such a situation?

III. PREREADING ACTIVITIES

The Prereading Activities which follow purpose to elicit *analogous* or *parallel* experiences from the reader's background so that he/she can identify more intensely with the *feelings* of the characters in the book—as they interact with other characters, situations, and events—as he/she reads and finds them familiar because they are but one step removed from the real occurrences in his/her life.

Name_____

Date_____

1. **What's Your IQ Score?**

   DIRECTIONS: What do YOU know about famous American inventors and discoverers? Go on an IQ (Inventor Quest) by matching the INVENTORS on the right to their INVENTIONS on the left. When you think you've found the right inventor, put his initials on the blank in front of the invention you believe he's responsible for. After you've finished your QUEST, you may want to see how well you scored by checking your matches in a good dictionary or encyclopedia. (Some of the inventors may have invented more than one thing listed on the left.)

   SCORING: 29 correct = GENIUS
   20–28 correct = SUPER
   12–19 correct = STRANGE
   3–11 correct = UNBELIEVABLE
   0–2 correct = WHEN THEY IN-
   VENTED THE WORD
   "dumb"—THEY HAD
   YOU IN MIND!

Inventions		Inventors
__POLAROID CAMERA	—1950s	Robert Fulton
__ELECTRIC RAZOR	—1931	Eli Whitney
__PARKING METER	—1935	Benjamin Franklin
__LIGHTNING ROD	—1752	Samuel F. B. Morse
__ELECTRIC TELEGRAPH	1832	Samuel Colt
__REVOLVER	—1835	William Hunt
__MACHINE GUN	—1862	Elisha G. Otis
__REPEATING RIFLE	—1860	O. F. Winchester
__BIFOCAL LENS	—1780	Richard J. Gatling
__COTTON GIN	—1792	Joseph F. Glidden
__TORPEDO	—1805	Melville R. Bissell
__COMMERCIAL		Alexander G. Bell
STEAMSHIP	—1807	Thomas A. Edison
__HELICOPTER	—1909	James Ritty
__ELEVATOR	—1852	John J. Loud
__SAFETY PIN	—1849	George Eastman
__STOVE WITH A "JACKET"		Whitcomb L. Judson
THAT PEOPLE CAN		King C. Gillette
STAND AROUND	—1742	Ole Evinrude
__BARBED WIRE	—1873	Igor Sikorsky
__CARPET SWEEPER	—1876	Jacob Schick
__MICROPHONE	—1876	Carlton C. Magee
—TELEPHONE	—1876	Edwin Land
__PHONOGRAPH	—1878	
__BALL-POINT PEN	—1888	
__KODAK CAMERA	—1888	
__ELECTRIC LAMP	—1879	
__MOTION PICTURES	—1893	
__ZIPPER	—1891	
__SAFETY RAZOR	—1895	
__OUTBOARD MOTOR	—1909	
__CASH REGISTER	—1879	

2. **WHO is WHO?**

> *DIRECTIONS: Below you will find a list of famous HIS-TORICAL PERSONAGES. Also, you will find a list of BYNAMES that can identify each historical person. (Some may have MORE THAN ONE byname.) When you find the nickname(s), write it opposite the real name of the famous HISTORICAL PERSON.*

FAMOUS HISTORICAL PERSONAGES

GEORGE WASHINGTON_____

PAUL REVERE_____

BENJAMIN FRANKLIN_____

THOMAS JEFFERSON_____

ABRAHAM LINCOLN_____

SUSAN B. ANTHONY_____

JOHN J. AUDUBON_____

GEORGE WASHINGTON

  CARVER _____

JOHN HANCOCK_____

BETSY ROSS_____

GEORGE M. PULLMAN_____

DANIEL WEBSTER _____

NOAH WEBSTER_____

WHO'S-WHO BY NAME

The Poor Richard
The Unlucky 16th
The "Big Wheel"
The Big French Spender
The Maxim-Maker
The Famous Nut Biggie
The Kite Flyer
The Great Emancipator
The Bird Man
The Five-Star Maker
The Honest One
The First U.S. Money-
  Maker
The Messenger
The Rights-Fights
  Leader
The Silver-Tongued
  Debater
The General
The Word Collector
The No. 1 Autographer

IV. POSTREADING DISCUSSION QUESTIONS

1. Amos *didn't like* a number of things about Ben Franklin. As you think about some of these, what might convince you that Amos' likes and dislikes are just about the same as yours?

2. While Amos felt that Ben had broken their *Agreement,* Ben was convinced that Amos had broken it! Why do you suppose Ben and Amos had such a *disagreement* about their *Agreement?*

3. How can you argue that Benjamin Franklin's inventions and/or discoveries were either from *practical need* or *curiosity?*

4. A *MAXIM* is defined as *the formulation of some principle or rule of behavior in a succinct way.* As you think about Benjamin Franklin's behavior in this book, and some of his maxims—*Waste not, want not; Early to bed, early to rise, makes a man healthy, wealthy, and wise; He that goes a borrowing goes a sorrowing; idleness and pride tax with a heavier hand than kings and parliaments*—why do you think that he does or doesn't practice what he preaches?

5. How can you explain the fact Amos understood and approved some of Ben's ideas such as the Franklin stove but ridiculed others such as the tide table, Poor Richard's maxims, and electricity?

6. In what ways do you think Amos' and Sophia's "war" was fought for nearly the same reasons as the American Revolutionary War with England?

V. HELPING CHILDREN TO REVEAL
THEIR COMPREHENSION

1.

The A.M.O.S.
Presidential Trophies

DIRECTIONS: Benjamin Franklin was eighty-three years old when George Washington became the first President of the United States in 1789. With the help of Red and Thomas Jefferson, Amos had little trouble persuading President Washington to hold an AWARDS BANQUET at which the guest of honor, Ben Franklin, would be presented TROPHIES recognizing the A.M.O.S.—Admirable Milestones Of Success—of each of his careers: author, printer, inventor, scientist, ambassador, and statesman. Under each of the A.M.O.S. Trophies below, briefly write what YOU would consider to be the most admirable reason for presenting Franklin the trophy.

WORLD'S BEST
Author

WORLD'S BEST
Printer

_____   _____

_____   _____

_____   _____

_____   _____

WORLD'S BEST
Inventor

WORLD'S BEST
Scientist

_____

_____

_____

_____

WORLD'S BEST
Ambassador

WORLD'S BEST
Statesman

_____

_____

_____

_____

Name_____

Date_____

2.

**AMOS' Scorecard!
or Setting
the Record
Straight!**

DIRECTIONS: It is well known that Ben Franklin said he wouldn't take any money for the invention of the Franklin stove. "I use inventions of men who lived before me," he explained. "Let other men use mine." But what of Amos? His involvement in and contributions to Ben's successes have been little known until now, and it's time YOU set the record straight! On the lines opposite each "AMOS-BEN" accomplishment below, spell out Amos' valuable contributions and what value each happening had for people around the world.

THE FIREPLACE CAPER:

_____

_____

_____

_____

_____

_____

_____

THE KITE CAPER:

_____

_____

_____

_____

_____

THE LIGHTNING ROD HAPPENING:

_____

_____

_____

THE POOR RICHARD VS. POOR AMOS CAPER:

_____

_____

_____

THE DECLARATION OF INDEPENDENCE CAPER:

_____

_____

_____

_____

_____

3.   **A View from the Hat**

DIRECTIONS: Amos got to know Ben Franklin well during the years he worked as the great man's associate and lived close to Franklin's idea-source in the old fur cap he wore constantly. From AMOS' point of view, how do you think he saw BENJAMIN FRANKLIN, idea man of many careers and talents? Put an X in the box in front of each of the statements below which you feel accurately REVEALS Amos' VIEWS of Ben.

☐ BEN BATHES IN A DANGEROUS AND UNSANITARY WAY.

☐ BEN IS DEPENDABLE AND GENEROUS.

☐ BEN SPENDS MOST OF HIS TIME ON UNIMPORTANT THINGS.

☐ MOST OF BEN'S SUCCESSES WERE ENTIRELY ACCIDENTAL.

☐ BEN DIDN'T CARE ABOUT THE PLIGHT OF THE MICE IN FRANCE.

☐ BEN RARELY PRACTICED THE MAXIMS OF POOR RICHARD.

☐ BEN'S GOOD SENSE COULD EASILY GO BAD WHEN PEOPLE MADE A BIG FUSS OVER HIM.

☐ BEN LIKES TO TORTURE MICE AND PEOPLE.

☐ BEN NEVER KEEPS HIS BARGAINS.

☐ WHEN BEN IS BEING A LADIES' MAN, HE IS PLAIN SILLY.

☐ BEN WAS AFRAID TO TAKE ME [AMOS] TO ENGLAND WITH HIM.

☐ ONE OF BEN'S AND MY [AMOS'] FAVORITE WAYS TO RELAX WAS KITE FLYING.

☐ WHEN BEN COULDN'T GET PEOPLE [AND MICE] TO DO WHAT HE WANTED THEM TO AGREE TO, HE WOULD TRICK THEM.

☐ BEN DID NOT KNOW HOW TO HANDLE HIS POPULARITY.

☐ BEN BECAME SO SEASICK ON THE BOAT TO FRANCE, HE DIDN'T HAVE A SINGLE IDEA THE ENTIRE TRIP.

☐ BEN DOESN'T THINK IT'S NECESSARY TO BE BUSY IN PEACETIME.

VI. RELATED-TO-READING EXPERIENCES

1. **Kite Capers**

   On page 58 you get a closeup view of the "Kite-mobile" which Ben invented for Amos. If you look closely, you also can see the "sail" rolled up along the side which Amos used to sail back up to the kite. Is this just a story, or CAN SUCH A THING REALLY WORK? Try to duplicate the prestorm fun which Amos had traveling up and down Franklin's kite string! Use a matchbox to make your "Amos-Car." Attach 4- to 6-inch thread to each of the four corners of the "car" and tie them to the "pulley"—made easily from a large paper clip. Another paper clip bent into the shape of a hook will hold the "Amos-Car" in place until it's in the air and you give the kite string several strong jerks to send it on its way down. If it's windy enough, an 8-inch square sail will carry the car back up. Your fun will be doubled if you make your own kite!

2. **Maxim March**

   Can you match maxims with Franklin? Abraham Lincoln, Will Rogers, and the Book of Proverbs (in the Bible) are good places to begin your personal collection of those that please you most.

3. Alphabet Antics

Amos has already given you the names of six of his brothers and sisters, and of course you know the oldest of the family: Amos! If you were going to name the rest, what would their names be? And, suppose each were going to give Ben Franklin, on his eighty-first birthday, a gift that also began with the same letter! What would the gift be?

Name		Gifts
Amos	A	
Bathsheba	B	
Claude	C	
Daniel	D	
	E	
	F	
	G	
	H	
	I	

Name		Gifts
	J	
	K	
	L	
	M	
	N	
	O	
	P	
	Q	

Name		Gifts
	R	
	S	
	T	
	U	
	V	
	W	
Xenophon	X	
Ysobel	Y	
Zenas	Z	

MR. REVERE AND I

Written and Illustrated by

ROBERT LAWSON

I. THE STORY

No haughtier stepper in the regiment than Scheherazade, no loftier-nosed champion of royalty and privilege. Naturally, the fall of this mare was equally great, even to the glue factory. And still more remarkable was the transformation which took place slowly but surely after Sam Adams talked her out of the glue cart and into the home of Paul Revere. Thus Sherry became the horse of a patriot, and soon knew all about the Revere family, the trade of the silversmith, and the doings of the Sons of Liberty. This is "An Account of certain Episodes in the Career of Paul Revere, Esq. as Revealed by his HORSE."

II. PREREADING DISCUSSION QUESTIONS

The questions which follow are illustrative of the kinds teachers can prepare for the purpose of releasing children to reveal how they feel *about some of the larger ideas and bigger meanings contained in the book* before it is read by the children.

About Royalty
1. How many different adjectives can you use that describe the traits, qualities, and the physical appearance of a *"person of royalty"*?
2. Why do you think so many people are impressed by *royalty*?

3. How do you define and/or identify:
   (a) a royal wedding? (b) a royal cat? (c) a royal ring?
   (d) a royal flower? (e) a royal gift? (f) royal treatment?
   (g) a royal appearance? (h) a royal mix-up? (i) a
   royal gown?

About Patriotism
4. How do you think it is possible for a person *today* to be
   considered both a REBEL and a PATRIOT at the
   same time?
5. What conditions might exist today wherein a United
   States citizen could be both a patriot and a traitor *at the
   same time?*
6. What things do you expect to hear in a *patriotic song?*
   What things do you expect to see in a *patriotic demon-
   stration?* What feelings do you expect to have after hear-
   ing a *patriotic speech?*

About Taxation
7. When people pay tax moneys, what do you believe they
   are *buying?*
8. How many different complaints have you heard people
   make about paying taxes?
9. What actions could today's taxpayers take if they disapprove of the ways they are represented when it
   comes to spending the dollars they pay in taxes?

III. PREREADING ACTIVITIES

The Prereading Activities which follow purpose to elicit *analogous* or *parallel* experiences from the reader's background so that
he/she can identify more intensely with the *feelings* of the characters in the book—as they interact with other characters, situations, and events—as he/she reads and finds them familiar because they are but one step removed from the real occurrences
in his/her life.

1. **"Dating" Historical Personages**

DIRECTIONS: Opposite the names of the famous historical personages listed below, write the MONTH, DATE, and YEAR for an EVENT, DEED, and/or THING closely associated with that person.

NAME	MONTH	DATE	YEAR	EVENT
George Washington				
King George III				
Samuel Adams				
John Adams				
Paul Revere				
James Otis				
Benjamin Franklin				
Nathan Hale				
John Hancock				

A ROYAL REACTIONNAIRE

DIRECTIONS: What do you believe about the attributes, characteristics, and behavior of a person of royal lineage? If you agree with the following statements, mark them "TRUE"; if you disagree, mark them "FALSE."

1. Where there's ROYALTY, there is wealth.　　　　　____True ____False

2. Failure, inconvenience, and unpleasantries are much harder for ROYALTY to endure than people like you and me.　　　　　____True ____False

3. A person of ROYALTY can be recognized by the way he/she talks.　　　　　____True ____False

4. A person of ROYALTY is easily upset by untidy conditions and imperfect things.　　　　　____True ____False

5. A person of ROYALTY finds it difficult to get along with people.　　　　　____True ____False

6. People of ROYALTY have long and unusual names.　　　　　____True ____False

7. People of ROYALTY make the best leaders.　　　　　____True ____False

IV. POSTREADING DISCUSSION QUESTIONS

1. Why do you think some people might misunderstand Paul Revere's mother's behavior over the English tea which the Sons of Liberty would not permit to be unloaded from the *Dartmouth?*
2. What do you believe are some of the main reasons why Scheherazade (Sherry) began to change her ideas about the Colonists' cause?
3. On page 40, Sam Adams says: *"Paul Revere needs a horse badly for his duties; you all know what* they *are."* Since it was well-known that Paul Revere was not a horseman (even Paul Revere himself, on page 46, admits he's never been on a horse), what ideas do you have that might explain what Sam Adams meant when he referred to *those duties?*
4. How would you agree or disagree with the idea that *pomp, ceremony,* and *naïveté* were enemies more dangerous to the British troops than the Minutemen?

5. After Leftenant Sir Cedric Barnstable recognized Scheherazade (p. 102) and accused Paul Revere of stealing her, Paul Revere found it necessary to move his family to Charlestown. Whether this incident between Leftenant Barnstable and Paul Revere and Ajax and Sherry actually ever took place the way the author, Robert Lawson, describes it is a matter of conjecture. However, the fact remains that Paul Revere did move his family away from Boston. Why do you suppose he made this decision? How do you suppose Paul Revere's famous ride might have been affected if he had not made this move at this time?

6. How would you try to explain Sherry's reasoning when she said (after recalling Ajax's statement on page 106: "Your master is your master"): *"Mr. Revere was no master—he was my loved and respected friend. We were not master and slave, we were partners, partners in a great new and shining adventure."*?

V. HELPING CHILDREN TO REVEAL
THEIR COMPREHENSION

1. **A Jekyll-Hyde Transformation**

SCHEHERAZADE: LOYALIST OR REBEL?

DIRECTIONS: From the very first, when Sherry says of herself:

To think that I, Scheherazade, once the most admired mount of the Queen's Own Household Cavalry, onetime toast of the Mustardshire Fencibles, late pride of His Royal Majesty's 14th Regiment of Foot, should be reduced to such a commonplace existence is somewhat saddening. **(P. 4.)**

one knows that this unusual horse will undergo some very confusing changes, encounter contradictory ideas and feelings, and eventually—as did many people in these years of the 1760s and 1770s—either remain loyal to the king or adopt the rebellious Colonial cause.

In front of each of SHERRY'S statements below, put an L if you believe the statement shows LOYALIST LEANINGS and an R if you think her comment shows her sympathies are favoring the COLONIALIST CAUSE.

1. _____Until that moment I had not fully realized how glorious it was to be free! Free of the everlasting monotony of barracks life, the deadly round of parade and drill, drill and parade . . . free of the brutal grooms, callous officers, stupid, overfed stablemates—like Ajax! (P. 103.)

2. _____While the work was not unduly hard the humiliation was almost too dreadful to bear. In the first place, for a horse of my background and attainments to be put in harness at all was unthinkable. (P. 36.)

3. _____Our food, moreover, was delicious and abundant. I must admit that these churlish peasants did raise excellent hay and grain, although the Royal Paymaster used to roar with pain at the prices he was charged. (P. 19.)

4. _____For the first time in my life I began to have doubts as to the divine wisdom of the King and his advisers. The glory of his Armed Forces, its Officers and Gentlemen, began to seem shoddy and tarnished. (P. 97.)

5. _____It all started with the imbecile, practically sacrilegious, determination of these stubborn Colonists to defy the sacred authority of our Royal and Sovereign Majesty King George III. (P. 4.)

6. _____I was horrified to see that these misguided Colonials were actually preparing for armed resistance to the King. Had it not been so serious it would have been laughable. (P. 59.)

7. _____Yet I had been brought up in the firm tradition that of all military crimes desertion was the very worst. I should have been horrified and outraged, but I could not be. (P. 55.)

8. _____As for me, a loyal subject of His Majesty, some of the things that were said fairly made my blood boil; on the other hand, some of their arguments made many of their grievances seem quite justified. (P. 51.)

9. _____It amused me to think of the far-reaching effects of our little ride to Portsmouth that cold winter night: the very King in London driven into a passion, General Gage in disfavor, his troops a laughingstock. (P. 109.)

10. _____Suddenly I saw a horse being hauled up to the yardarm and lowered into the black hold of a transport. It was Ajax. He had proved a false friend, a stupid and bitter enemy, but remembering the horrors of those transports perhaps I should have been moved to feel some pity for him. . . . I was not moved, but whinnied long and gleefully. (P. 151).

2.   **The Many Hats of Paul Revere**

HATS 'N' HAPPENINGS

DIRECTIONS: Paul Revere generally is remembered by two of the many hats he wore as a Colonialist: A fine silversmith and a patriot who rode through the countryside warning the people that "the British were out." But, as any reader of Mr. Revere and I *knows, Mr. Revere wore "many hats" for the many different kinds of happenings in which he was involved. In each of the "HATS" below, write in a different Paul Revere talent. Then, under each hat, briefly describe the incident or happening to support your "talent-scout" ideas.*

FIRE WARDEN	ENGRAVER
BLACKSMITH	SILVERSMITH
DENTIST	HORSEMAN
ARTIST	SHARPSHOOTER
ACTOR	FARRIER
PATRIOT	SPY

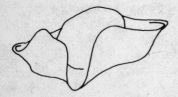

_____

_____

_____

_____

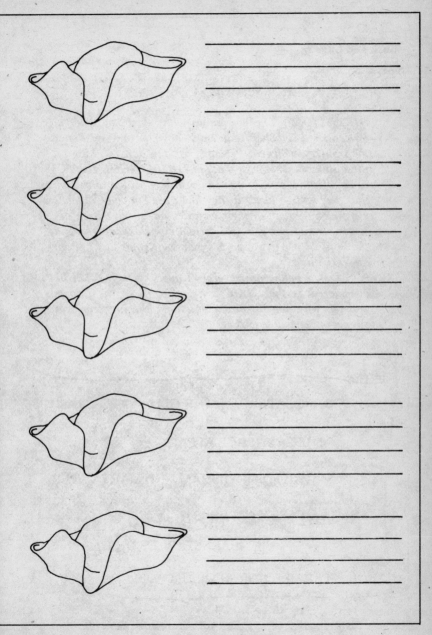

Luck and Liberty

HORSESHOE LUCK

DIRECTIONS: The new shoes with which the colonial farrier shod Scheherazade must have been even better than Sherry believed. Perhaps, for the Sons of Liberty, these shoes had some of that old "HORSESHOE LUCK" in them which cause some superstitious people to believe that they will be lucky if they find one. For the Colonists were lucky! Many of their victories might have been defeats if it had not been for certain coincidences—or, did the Sons of Liberty "cause" their own good luck? What do YOU think?

Listed below are several "Capers" which could be considered as sheer LUCK. Select some of the Capers and tell why you do or do not think the outcome was simply unbelievable LUCK!

THE SKUNK CAPER   THE GLUE-CART CRASH

THE LOST-RACE AFFAIR

THE FORT WILLIAM AND MARY CAPER

THE TEA-PARTY CAPER

BARNSTABLE'S DICE CAPER

THE OLD NORTH SPIRE CAPER

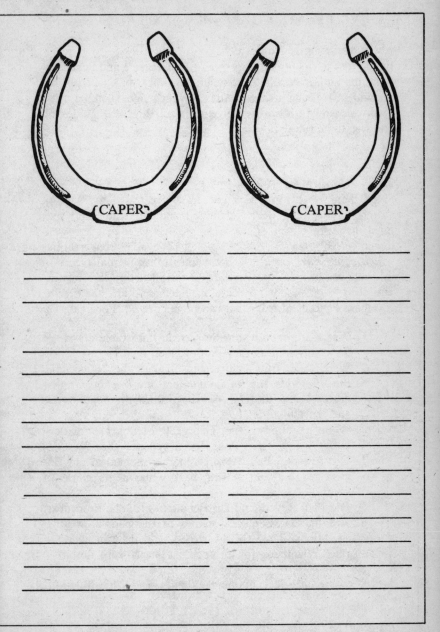

CAPER

CAPER

_____
_____
_____

_____
_____
_____
_____
_____
_____
_____
_____
_____
_____

VI. RELATED-TO-READING EXPERIENCES

1. Mapping the Routes

In addition to the famous last ride of Paul Revere and Scheherazade, the author details three other rides they took (see pp. 65, 78, and 90). Using a current atlas as your guide, sketch a 1768 map which might have been given to Paul Revere to guide him on these three rides.

2. Historical Fact Finder

Since there were no tape recorders to record conversations, writers of historical works of fiction and nonfiction find they must do a great deal of research into the *facts* that are well-documented, then invent plausible, believable conversations *which could have occurred.* Sometimes other factual pieces of information, needed by writers of historical fiction, are missing and need to be supplied by careful imagination and the piecing together of pieces of truth that can be uncovered. For example:

1. Was there a Leftenant Sir Cedric Barnstable and were his front teeth as Lawson described them?
2. Were there four escort ships named the *Implacable,* the *Incapable,* the *Impossible,* and the *Implausible* that accompanied the two transport ships the *Thunderous* and the *Unfathomable?*
3. While it is known that George Washington wore dentures, is it true that Paul Revere repaired them?
4. Is it true that Paul Revere's mother seemed to put English tea and her sewing basket above the cause of liberty?
5. Did Paul Revere and Dr. Benjamin Franklin ever meet?
6. Are the dates, places, names of the people, weather conditions, names of the streets, and the like all accurate? Was there, for instance, an Old North Church?

Do some historical snooping! What is fact? What is fiction?

THE ANIMAL FAMILY
by RANDALL JARRELL

Illustrated by Maurice Sendak

I. THE STORY

In a place where the forest ran down to the ocean, a hunter lived all alone. It was a beautiful place. The Spring meadow was foam white and the sea blue with flowers. The sun dipped into the sea at night, and meteors streaked across the sky. But there was no one to give the flowers to and no one to whom the hunter could say, "Look! Look!"—until he found room in his rustic cabin and in his heart for a family. And a strange and wonderful family it was. First came the lovely singing mermaid. Then, Old-Eat-and-Sleep, the bear. And a lynx with a purr like distant thunder. And finally, a shipwrecked human baby boy. *"Say what you like, but such things do happen—not often, but they do happen."* Taking time takes one into timelessness. Thus the story seems to be without beginning and without an end in the sense that one is aware of its existence long before the flyleaf and long after the final page.

II. PREREADING DISCUSSION QUESTIONS

The questions which follow are illustrative of the kinds which teachers can prepare for the purpose of releasing children to reveal how they feel *about some of the larger ideas and bigger meanings contained in the book* before it is read by the children.

About Happiness
1. What kinds of things do people want which they believe will make them happy?
2. Some people are sure some things will bring them happiness but, after they have them, they still feel unhappy. What reasons can you think of that might explain why this could happen?
3. What do you think are the ten most common reasons for *unhappiness* in young people?
4. What do you think are some of the things that make *being alone* so difficult for a young person?

About Love
5. Sometimes it is easier to let someone know that you love him/her by the things that you *do,* that is, by *showing* that you do. How do young people *show* their love, not by words, but by the things they do?
6. Frequently people will suffer many hardships for those they love. How many different examples can you give for why this happens?
7. Most people like to have a friend with whom they can share ideas. What specific things do close friends talk about, show, confide, and/or help each other with?

About Boredom and Leisure Time
8. What situation can you tell about which shows a time you were *very bored?* Where was it? Who was there? What caused the situation?
9. Almost everyone has had to stay indoors at one time or other due to illness or bad weather. What activities do you do to make the time pass during these times?

About Animals and Pets
10. You have probably seen on television or read or heard stories about the problems that occur when someone

makes a pet out of a wild animal. What do you think are some of these problems?

11. How many different ways can you think of that would show how people *really love* the pets they have and *really do* everything to make them happy *as animals* in a human world?

12. What do you think you could do to make an animal just as comfortable living with you as it would be living in its natural environment?

III. PREREADING ACTIVITIES

The Prereading Activities which follow purpose to elicit *analogous* or *parallel* experiences from the reader's background so that he/she can identify more intensely with the *feelings* of the characters in the book—as they interact with other characters, situations, and events—as he/she reads and finds them familiar because they are but one step removed from the real occurrences in his/her life.

Animal Capers

DIRECTIONS: There are people who notice HUMAN traits or qualities about animals and tell very-difficult-to-believe stories about the kinds of near-human things different animals can do. Of the pets (or other animals) you've known or heard about, which ones can you put in the blanks below?

AN ANIMAL WHO IS ABLE TO . . .

1. DANCE, such as _____

2. ROB or STEAL, such as _____

3. REMEMBER, such as _____

4. TALK, such as _____

5. PLAY HUMAN GAMES, such as_____

6. WORK FOR MONEY, such as_____

7. FIGHT IN A WAR, such as _____

8. TAKE A BATH, such as _____

9. UNDERSTAND HUMAN SPEECH, such as

_____

10. BECOME A MOVIE (TV) STAR, such as

_____

2. **Animal Habits and Habitats**

> *DIRECTIONS: As anyone who has ever visited a well-kept zoo knows, the animals there are kept in an environment as nearly like their NATURAL HOMES as possible. Suppose one summer you rented an old barn on the outskirts of the city and charged people for a PET-SITTING SERVICE: "Any animal cared for and made happy" is your slogan. BUT YOU NEVER EXPECTED A BOOMING BUSINESS OF SUCH UNUSUAL PETS! Your idea of keeping them well and happy means that you will—as best you can—provide a NATURAL HABITAT for each, teach them to live together, and to TOLERATE each other's normal habits. For each of the below-listed animals left in your care, what will you need to do?*

THE ANIMALS	FOOD	EATING HABITS	SLEEPING HABITS	NORMAL BEHAVIOR TO BE WARY OF
bear club				
corn snake				
barn owl				
alligator				
penguin				
chimpanzee				
eagle				
lynx				
dog				

49

IV. POSTREADING DISCUSSION QUESTIONS

1. The sea people felt sorry for the mermaid and called her "the one who lives with the animals." Why do you think they felt this way about her?

2. What growing-up differences did you notice among the bear, the lynx, and the boy?

3. For long periods of time, the mermaid never seemed to feel she needed to say anything. Why do you think this bothered the hunter?

4. What possible reasons can you give that might explain why the boy continued to play *"The-Lynx-Found-Me"* game with his parents? What do you suppose the boy really believed about his birth?

5. Why do you suppose the mermaid didn't seem angered, afraid, or alarmed that the hunter, with deerskins and seal-skins on the floor, bearskins as a bed cover, lion fur as a cloak, and sea-otter skin as a cap, *killed animals to provide for himself?*

6. When you think about the ways the bear and the lynx grew up, how do you think it might be possible for the hunter to feel that the bear's growing-up period was just one *"long accident"?*

7. So many people today seem to feel uncomfortable about being different! In communities, schools, and families, people say we must try to get along together *in spite of our differences!* How would you try to argue that the love and close, harmonious family living that was present in *The Animal Family* was a result of their being different?

8. When raising the mermaid, the sea people taught her that *everything good comes from the sea and, in the end, everything comes back to the sea.* What arguments do you think some people might make if they chose to try to convince the mermaid that she was not taught correctly? What arguments do you think the sea people would use to prove that they were right?

V. HELPING CHILDREN TO REVEAL
THEIR COMPREHENSION

Name_____

Date_____

1. ## Loving DIFFERENCES

DIRECTIONS: As with all close families, each member of THE ANIMAL FAMILY had certain habits, feelings, and ways of living and growing which the others needed to understand and adjust to. As the Hunter's family grew, he discovered the wonderful natural differences of each and learned to love and live with them. Under each member of the Hunter's family pictured below, cut out and paste the UNIQUE DIFFERENCES you believe the Hunter particularly associates with each.

GOES AWAY TO SLEEP	GOES AWAY FROM TROUBLES	SWEET TOOTH	LOVES TO ROCK 'N' ROLL
GROWS SLOWLY	TOUGH BOXER	SHELL COLLECTOR	SUPER FOOD GATHERER
DOESN'T GET BORED	MAKES UP SEA STORIES	HATES SWEETS	THE FAMILY WASHCLOTH

2.   **A Family Party**

DIRECTIONS: You have been invited to a family party at the Hunter's cabin in the wilderness! Even though you are a stranger, you would like to make them feel at ease and accept you as a close friend. You go on a wild shopping spree and manage to get each a most appropriate present. And, since they don't have names as we do, you have to use a nickname which identifies a personality characteristic you remember from the story. Opposite each of the characters below, write in the nickname and the gift you brought for each one. You may choose your presents from the "GIFT LIST" and your nicknames from the "NAME LIST" below—or, use your own ideas.

	Nickname	*Gift*
THE HUNTER		
THE MERMAID		
THE BEAR		
THE LYNX		
THE BOY		

Name List	*Gift List*
Eat-and-Sleep	Large Honeycomb
Patient One	Red Seashells
Liquid Voice	Salt Water
Kneady-Paws	Lace Handkerchief
Game Player	Live Rabbits
Toymaker	Tennis Ball
Featherhead	Swim Fins
Swim Teacher	Nuts and Berries
Bee-Teaser	Sea People Language Book
Ballplayer	Maple Leaves and Wild Flowers

3. **THE MERMAID'S Metamorphosis**

DIRECTIONS: The mermaid was the first of the sea people ever to travel so far from the sea and stay so long away—LIVING WITH ANIMALS. As she became a part of the ANIMAL FAMILY, *she needed to learn many new things and change her ideas, feelings, language, and behavior. Some of these NEW things were simply additional pieces of information (burning coals are hot), while others were CHANGES she made because she now lived with animals.*

Below are some statements about the Mermaid. In front of the ones which you think show that the Mermaid CHANGED after becoming part of the Animal Family, put a C. In front of those which simply show NEW IN-FORMATION ABOUT LAND DWELLERS which she learned, put an I.

_____ 1. Sweet things taste terrible.

_____ 2. The land is better than the sea because it continually changes.

_____ 3. Death is a heartbreaking occurrence.

_____ 4. Cooked meat is unappetizing.

_____ 5. Boredom results when you don't have new things to think of.

_____ 6. Some animals grow fast; some grow very slowly.

_____ 7. Flowers look like beautiful shells.

_____ 8. Fresh water tastes hollow; salt water is better to drink.

_____ 9. Thinking in the Hunter's language.

_____10. Knowing all the nursery rhymes by heart.

_____11. Being alone is very difficult.

_____12. Tears come when there is great joy or sadness.

VI. RELATED-TO-READING EXPERIENCES

1. **Word Hunt**

   The author uses words vividly to describe some of the sounds the animals make as well as the characteristic ways they move. Words such as whining, liquid voice, growling, purring, snoring, grunting, scratching, rubbing, padding, and so forth. What others can you find? Which animal do these sounds and motions belong to?

2. **Feline Fun**

   How many different members of the *cat family* can you find? On 3″ X 5″ cards, record all the information you can on one side and a picture (sketch, cutout, or photo) on the other. Perhaps some of your friends who are cat-lovers will become interested and you can begin a trading card swapping and collection contest.

3. **Escapes from Boredom**

   Most people are able to make the best of the boring situations in which they frequently find themselves. In as many of the situations as you can list below, find out from different people how they "escape" from these boring circumstances.

BORING SITUATIONS	ESCAPE ARTIST #1	ESCAPE ARTIST #2	ESCAPE ARTIST #3
1. Standing in line.			
2. A long trip.			
3. Having to listen to a story for the umpteenth time.			
4. Being sent to bed early.			
5. Having to sit and listen to a lesson in school which you already know.			
6. Having to sit and listen to a speech or sermon which you don't understand.			
7. Having to sit politely with adults while they talk about things which don't interest you.			

THE RESCUERS
by MARGERY SHARP

Illustrated by Garth Williams

I. THE STORY

At a meeting of that venerable organization of mice, the Prisoners' Aid Society, it is decided that the most important item on the autumn program is the rescue of a Norwegian poet from the dungeon of the Black Castle. The first step, the society agrees, is to find a linguist who knows not only the universal mouse language but Norwegian as well. The fabulous Miss Bianca is the obvious choice to secure such a mouse, living as she does at the Embassy and being free to travel in the Diplomatic Bag.

Miss Bianca then secures the services of Nils, a stalwart Norwegian seafaring mouse, and her part of the mission is over. But though her high breeding and luxurious life-style have made her somewhat timid, she cannot resist joining Nils and Bernard, the brave and love-smitten pantry mouse, on their adventure to the Black Castle. There they encounter Mamelouk, the vulgar, fiendish prison cat, who almost brings their rescue efforts to an abrupt, grisly halt.

II. PREREADING DISCUSSION QUESTIONS

The questions which follow are illustrative of the kinds which teachers can prepare for the purpose of releasing children to re-

56

veal how they feel *about some of the larger ideas and bigger meanings contained in the book* before it is read by the children.

About First Impressions

1. How does a person gain *first impressions* of the people he/she meets?
2. What has been your experience about the accuracy or inaccuracy of the first impressions you have formed about certain people?
3. What do you think you might do to keep from having a first impression that would be unfair or unkind or hard to get rid of?
4. Besides people, what other things have you had first impressions or hunches about? How did they turn out? That is, at first did you think you would like or dislike them, and did you still feel the same way after the *first* impression wore off?

About Feelings

5. Sometimes young people can be cruel to each other by making fun. You can probably recall a time when you have been cruel to someone by making fun of him/her, by calling him/her a name, or by teasing him/her in some way. Why do you think people do this? What causes you to do it? How would you describe the way you felt when you were the victim?
6. Why do you think some people believe that, if a person has been mistreated, that person in turn becomes more sensitive to the feelings of others?
7. Feeling useless, unwanted, too weak or too small or too young; or, being too poor, or from the wrong side of the tracks is something most people have experienced at least once. Think about such a time. What were your innermost feelings?

About Rescue Missions

8. How many *different* situations can you describe in which people have found themselves involved in unusual rescue attempts?

III. PREREADING ACTIVITIES

The Prereading Activities which follow purpose to elicit *analogous* or *parallel* experiences from the reader's background so that he/she can identify more intensely with the *feelings* of the characters in the book—as they interact with other characters, situations, and events—as he/she reads and finds them familiar because they are but one step removed from the real occurrences in his/her life.

1. **Animal Clubs**

IF YOU COULD TALK TO THE ANIMALS

DIRECTIONS: Suppose that the following animals had SECRET ORGANIZATIONS, each with a single purpose. If you could talk to these different groups, what CAUSE or PURPOSE that you feel would be most appropriate to their species would you try to convince them to adopt which would be most helpful to human beings on this planet?

For example: An organization of DOVES might meet to plan ways to convince the nations of the world to adopt a WORLD FLAG—rainbow colored with a large white DOVE in the center.

ANIMAL SPECIES	CLUB'S PURPOSE
1. bees	
2. dogs	
3. mice	
4. lions	
5. elephants	
6. cats	
7. turtles	
8. monkeys	

2. **Mission: Rescue**

MISSION: POSSIBLE!

DIRECTIONS: In the cruel country of Leurc, ruled by a vicious dictator, King Suoiciv, high on top of a mountain there is an escape-proof White Prison. Each cell has a prisoner serving a sentence because he/she has displeased King Suoiciv.

Your mission, should you decide to accept it, is to

PUNISHMENT PRIORITY	RESCUE PRIORITY

get into *White Prison* and free these *TEN MOST-WANTED* people. *Before you decide how you will go about it, you need to decide (1) whose imprisonment was the most unjust and (2) what priority you will give to the rescue of each.*

In the boxes in front of each of the ten prisoners, place numbers from 1 to 10 to indicate (1) the least just to the most just punishment and (2) the person you would rescue first to the person you would rescue last.

PRISONER'S NAME/AGE	CRIME and PUNISHMENT
Sheila Noshoes Age 16	Refuses to wear shoes at anytime. 10 years.
Lavender Blue Age 23	Artist paints only with purple. 33 years.
Nappy Hare Age 14	Boy who has shoulder-length hair. 21 years.
Enda Rope Age 47	Tried to strangle a prison guard. 99 years.
Ima Kleervu Age 11	Student who cheated on a test. 15 years.
Shott Gunne Age 29	Killed King Suoiciv's brother. 71 years.
Timie Gulp Age 7	Refuses to drink milk. 11 years.
Case d'Joint Age 66	Hungry man who stole a box of crackers. 3 years.
Ibee Dumme Age 9	Boy who won't learn to read. 57 years.
Rocky Rolle Age 35	Tuba player who plays only rock music. 83 years.

IV. POSTREADING DISCUSSION QUESTIONS

1. Miss Bianca, a most sheltered and unlikely mouse to be of value on a rescue mission in Black Castle, proved to have the needed talents at the right time to make the rescue a success. As you think about Miss Bianca's role in this mission, what can you remember about her which contributed to the liberation of the Norwegian poet?

2. Although Miss Bianca, Nils, and Bernard were as determined as they were clever, much of their success came from a *fourth* helper: "Lady Luck!" What happened in the story which you consider examples of unbelievable good luck?

3. Miss Bianca, Nils, and Bernard are mice and never did things that mice could not do, although the author gave them the ability to *think and feel* as human beings. What human characteristics do you think they possessed that are similar to the thoughts and feelings of people you know today?

4. Why do you suppose some readers of this book would argue that Mamelouk, the cat, *actually helped* rather than hindered the poet's rescue?

5. If Madam Chairwoman had presented a "Job Description" to the full meeting of the Prisoners' Aid Society, describing the persons needed to liberate the poet from Black Castle (keeping Nils and Bernard in mind now that you know them well), what qualities would she have suggested they look for?

V. HELPING CHILDREN TO REVEAL THEIR COMPREHENSION

1. Mouse Medals

There are so many different medals because each one has a *different purpose*. While some medals are named after people (like the Newbery Award medal, named after John Newbery and given annually to the author of the best children's book for that year), other medals are named for other appropriate reasons. Almost always, there's an inscription on the medal, indicating succinctly why it is given.

MEDAL MAKERS

DIRECTIONS: *Below are five Mouse Medals, each one presented to a mouse for certain heroic deeds. While each one has been named, only one, the Tybalt Star, has had an inscription written for it: "For Gallantry in Face of Cats." Write appropriate inscriptions for the other four in the space provided. Then, under each, place the names of the mice to whom you think the medals should be given.*

THE GOLD MOUSE-HEART MEDAL

THE TYBALT STAR MEDAL

"For Gallantry in Face of Cats"

THE JEAN FROMAGE MEDAL

THE NILS–MISS BIANCA MEDAL

THE COPPER-BOOT MEDAL

2. Operation Plan

As you know, from the very beginning when Madam Chairwoman announced to the Prisoners' Aid Society that they *would* rescue the Norwegian poet, there was very little doubt in her mind that they would succeed. But WHO? HOW? WHEN? Unlike the television show, "Mission Impossible," nothing was preplanned; instead, problems were allowed to pop up, one by one, and solved in the same manner.

Suppose you were the old, rheumatic mouse (p. 4) who had spent six weeks, unsuccessfully, in Black Castle and, knowing what you know of all the problems and dangers, *how would you preplan the Norwegian poet's rescue from beginning to end* from Miss Bianca's "map" to the raft in the river? Use the Official Prisoners' Aid Society Mouse-Plan Form below:

PROBLEM SITUATION	MICE INVOLVED	PROBLEM SOLUTION
1.		
2.		
3.		
4.		
5.		

3. A Poet's Song

Once rescued, the young Norwegian poet used his best talent to thank the Prisoners' Aid Society and reward their fine and noble work by leaving his "Ballad from Norway" for all the world to know and sing for centuries of mouse generations to come. On the music paper below, complete the poet's ballad that retells the whole rescue story from the Moot-house to the Porcelain Pagoda.

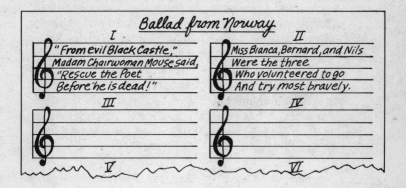

VI. RELATED-TO-READING EXPERIENCES

1. **Newspaper Research**
    By researching through as many daily newspapers as you can, cut out all articles you can find that remind you of any of the ideas, incidents, or characters you remember from *The Rescuers*. For example, people being rescued, stolen items recovered, prison stories, animal heroes and heroines, and so forth. Prepare a scrapbook or bulletin board display called: THE RESCUERS: IN FACT & FICTION. Under or next to each newspaper item, write a sentence or two which points out a similar character or happening from the fictional book.

2. **Checking Sexist Feelings**
    While *The Rescuers* was written by a well-known woman writer, ideas and feelings about male-female stereotyping

have changed radically since 1959. Below are a number of exact quotes from the book. Some readers think that it was necessary, in several instances, to picture Miss Bianca as an extremely female stereotype or else much of the charm and humor in the story would have been lost. Others think such comments were absolutely unnecessary and prosexist. Still others think that some of the statements were neither pro- nor antisexist—"just part of the story." What do you think? Place a check ($\sqrt{}$) in front of each statement you think is definitely sexist and unnecessary. Put a double check ($\sqrt{}\sqrt{}$) if you think the statement is sexist, but necessary to the story. Finally, put an 0 in front of each statement which you think has no sexist significance at all.

1._____"No one more than I," said the Secretary, "admires Madam Chairwoman's spirit. But has she, in her feminine enthusiasm, considered the difficulties?" (P. 8.)

2._____"That remains to be seen," said Madam Chairwoman. She had indeed some doubts herself; but she also had great faith in her own sex. (P. 11.)

3._____However sheltered, all women have certain domestic instincts. (P. 26.)

4._____It has often been remarked that women of rank, once their affections are engaged, can be completely reckless of the consequences. (P. 33.)

5._____Miss Bianca shuddered. —But in the morning, neither Nils nor Bernard said a word about it, and with a mixture of relief and irritation she concluded that they had just been playing a masculine game, like golf. (P. 84.)

6._____"You and Nils make your plans," said Miss Bianca gently; "aren't they dangerous too? You have strength and agility; I—" she looked modestly down again— "have only charm. You must allow me to employ it." (P. 98.)

7._____". . . yet Miss Bianca's instinct was right too: there is nothing like housework for calming the nerves. (P. 120.)

A WRINKLE IN TIME
by MADELEINE L'ENGLE

I. THE STORY

It was a dark and stormy night; Meg Murry, her small brother
Charles Wallace, and her mother had come down to the kitchen
for a midnight snack when they were upset by the arrival of a
most disturbing stranger.

"*Wild nights are my glory,*" *the unearthly stranger told
them.* "*I just got caught in a downdraft and blown off course.
. . . I shall just sit down for a moment, . . . and then I'll be on
my way. Speaking of ways, by the way, there* is *such a thing as a
tesseract.*" (A *tesseract,* in case the reader doesn't know, is a
wrinkle in time.) Meg's father, a physicist working for the
government and in a top-secret, classified position, had dis-
appeared. Charles Wallace, at age five, has the uncanny ability
to know his mother's and Meg's thoughts almost before they
do. Then, there is the *un*haunted, old shingled house at the edge
of the woods, inhabited by three unusual women, one of which
admits taking twelve sheets from the constable's wife.

II. PREREADING DISCUSSION QUESTIONS

*The questions which follow are illustrative of the kinds which
teachers can prepare for the purpose of releasing children to reveal how* they feel *about some of the larger ideas and bigger
meanings contained in the book* before it is read by the children.

About Feelings of Low Self-Worth

1. What things do you think would cause a young person to feel inferior to others?

2. Suppose someone you care very much about is convinced that he/she is dumb, repulsive, and unattractive, but you know this is *not* true! Since your friend won't believe what even you say, what would you attempt to do to help this person think better of himself/herself?

3. Think about a time when *nothing went right* no matter how hard you tried or what you did. What was the occasion? Who was involved? What did you do? What happened? Whose fault was it? How did one sad situation seem to lead to another . . . and another?

About Disguising One's Feelings

4. Think about two events in your life when (1) you were extremely happy because you received something or because something fantastic happened to you, and (2) you were painfully sad and miserable because of the worst misfortune or bad luck that could have happened to you at that time. To top it off, you had to continue your daily activities, talk and work with the people you see every day in spite of these events. In both situations, what did you do to hide your feelings from other people who were close to you and knew you very well? How successful were you? What "tattled" on you? What did you find hardest to do?

5. When someone is telling you something unpleasant or boring, or giving you advice or information you don't wish to hear, very often you will *shut your mind to what they are saying,* even though you couldn't cover your ears to keep the "unwanted sounds" out. What devices and/or tricks did you use to keep your mind closed? What did the person do to try to *open you up* when he/she realized he/she wasn't getting through to you?

About Sameness and Difference

6. Suppose there were a large nation in the world called *Bliss* where the government took care of all of the worries it is possible for Man to have. In Bliss, everyone is the same, does the same thing, in the same way, at the same time; eats the same food, lives in a house the same as all other houses, works the same number of hours, and so forth. "We are happy in Bliss," says the leader, "because we are all alike. Differences create problems so we've eliminated all difference!" What would you want to consider before deciding to become a citizen of Bliss?

7. What things can you think of that young people do to *stand out* from others? What do your friends do to keep from becoming conspicuous so they are "like everyone else"?

8. Why do you suppose people want to be different from everyone else on some occasions and the same on others?

9. What pro or con argument would you give concerning the idea that a person *sacrifices his/her individuality* when he enters a contest or tries to solve problems in the "right" way set forth by his teacher, even though he obtains accurate solutions through his own way of working?

III. PREREADING ACTIVITIES

The Prereading Activities which follow purpose to elicit *analogous* or *parallel* experiences from the reader's background so that he/she can identify more intensely with the *feelings* of the characters in the book—as they interact with other characters, situations, and events—as he/she reads and finds them familiar because they are but one step removed from the real occurrences in his/her daily life.

1. **Fantastic Foibles!**
   DIRECTIONS: The weirdest thing possible happened to you this morning as you looked in the mirror! As you stood there gazing, words began to appear. When the writing stopped you discover your three worst weaknesses printed on the glass in front of you. At first, you're angry, then ashamed; but as the day begins (and before it ends at midnight), you find out that your three weaknesses turn out to be your most valuable strengths for dealing with the unexpected events of the day. List your three greatest weaknesses, then write yourself into a situation where these three things turned out to be the most valuable strengths you could possess!

   For example: WEAKNESSES: (1) *telling lies,* (2) *acting without thinking,* (3) *crying whenever something goes wrong.*

   On your way back to school after lunch, you see two men with guns about to go into a bank, but they see you and know that you spotted them. They decide that the only thing for them to do is to take you into the bank with them and make you a part of the holdup! . . . *Now, finish the story by using your weaknesses to prevent the robbery.*

2. **If Wishes Came True . . .**
   As we watch the news on television or take notice of all the things happening around us, we are inclined to make *wishes* to solve those problems and wrongs which we observe. However, if we stopped to think about it, *we could be in worse trouble* if all these wishes were granted. Notice the list of wishes below. Think about each one carefully. What if each one came true? Would it be a good thing for the world? If so, write the word *good* on the blank under the wish. If you have some doubts that such a wish, if it came true, would cause a chain reaction of *worse* events, write in what your predictions would be.

1. If everyone had a college degree, there wouldn't be any poor or out-of-work people.

_____

_____

2. If every adult were given the same amount of money each week (including the President), everyone would have an equal chance in life.

_____

_____

3. If children weren't forced to go to school, schools would be happier, better, safer places.

_____

_____

4. If everyone always told nothing but the truth, then lying and cheating would be wiped out.

_____

_____

5. If there were no weapons of any kind in the world, there would be no more killings and no more wars.

_____

_____

6. If everyone had the same strength, skills, and mental ability, there would be no more inequality.

_____

_____

IV. POSTREADING DISCUSSION QUESTIONS

1. On page 7, Meg is feeling very sorry for herself and asks: *"Why must everything happen to me?"* How might you explain to Meg that it *could be all her fault* that "everything always happens to her"?

2. A number of things caused Meg to have a negative view of herself: her twin brothers; her physicist father with more than one Ph.D.; a mother who was gorgeous and a bright scientist; a mouthful of braces; thick glasses; no friends; and a lousy reputation for being a poor student and a difficult discipline problem in school. If you tried to sort out these things with Meg in an attempt to get her to think a bit more positively, what would you say to her?

3. When the Happy Medium (pp. 86-87) showed Meg, Calvin, and Charles Wallace the planet Earth, they were fearful and sickened when they saw the beauty of the Earth shadowed by the Dark Thing. When Meg asked if the Dark Thing had just come recently, Mrs. Whatsit replied:

   "No, Meg. It hasn't just come. It has been there for a great many years. That is why your planet is such a troubled one."

   Probably there's no *one* thing that Mrs. Whatsit refers to, but many. Suppose you had *tessered* yourself several million light-years off and saw your planet Earth in the shadow of the Dark Thing. What would be your guesses as to the things that have created this evil, awful shadow?

4. On page 30, Charles Wallace points out clearly why he's afraid to learn to read: he doesn't want to be hated. What specific examples can you give that would show that Charles Wallace could be right about the way he feels?

5. If nothing else, Meg knew her own faults very well, even though she didn't seem to be able to do anything about any of them. She was impatient, couldn't hide her feelings, and lacked moderation, to name three. Explain how you now can agree with Mrs. Whatsit when she advised Meg that these faults would come in handy on Camazotz.

6. How is it possible to say that IT was without *love* when it cared for and made sure that everyone on Camazotz had everything needed for peace and security?

7. Everyone has a "Black Thing" to fight, although probably no two people have exactly the same "Black Thing" to fight. How many examples of Black Things can you suggest?

8. Aunt Beast, who cannot see, states (p. 186), *"We look not at the things which are what you would call seen, but at the things which are not seen. For the things which are seen are temporal. But the things which are not seen are eternal."* What specific examples can you cite that would support Aunt Beast's comment?

V. HELPING CHILDREN TO REVEAL
THEIR COMPREHENSION

Name_____

Date_____

1. | **Character Composites**

DIRECTIONS: *Suppose each of the major characters in the story represents something which, to some extent, can be found in each of us . . . making us all COMPOSITES of many different traits. Under each of the silhouettes below, write in what you believe to be the trait particularly unique to each and which, to some degree, is found in all of us.*

The desire to shape others' lives

Powers of ESP (extrasensory perception)

Shutting out ugliness

Wisdom

Half in and half out of reality

Fear

Uncontrolled emotions

Understanding sensitivity

Powerful command of communication

Love

Hate

Selfishness

Pride

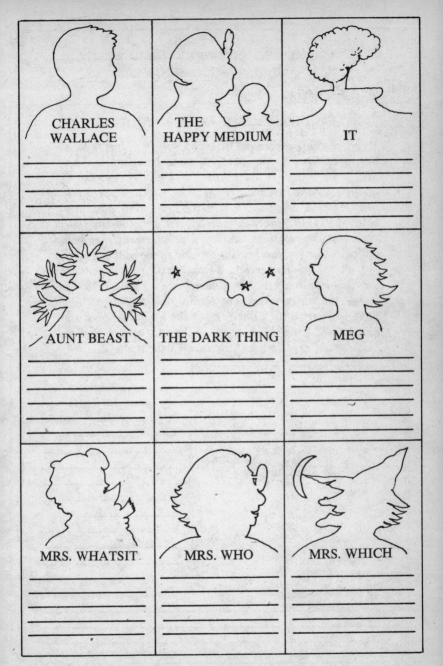

CHARLES WALLACE

THE HAPPY MEDIUM

IT

AUNT BEAST

THE DARK THING

MEG

MRS. WHATSIT

MRS. WHO

MRS. WHICH

2. **Blast-off to Camazotz**

INSIDE MY SPACE COAT POCKET . . .

Meg's rescue mission has failed! First Dr. Murry, then Calvin tessered to the planet Camazotz to try to help Meg free Charles Wallace from IT. Only six hours ago, Mission Control contacted you, flew you to Cape Kennedy, Florida, and now TEN MINUTES before a historic blast-off for the planet Camazotz, you are alone in your space capsule as the countdown progresses. Then you notice . . . one of the pockets in your space coat is empty . . . and as you realize this, Mrs. Whatsit materializes in the cabin and offers you your choice of any THREE people or things which she would miniaturize for you until you arrive on Camazotz. What would you choose to take with you? Draw them in the Space Coat Pocket below, then explain why you selected them.

VI. RELATED-TO-READING EXPERIENCES

1.   **Charles Wallace Tessers and Transforms!**
Cut out the rectangle below. You will notice Charles
Wallace grinning at you on the right. On the heavy black
line in the middle, fold the left-hand side back and
under Charles Wallace. Next, put a little glue around
the inside edges to hold Charles Wallace steady while
you help him TESSER! The dotted (_ _ _ _) lines will
show you how to help Charles Wallace TESSER by
folding them in as many "wrinkles" (both forward and
backward) as you can. As you will see, CHARLES
WALLACE IS AN AMAZING CHILD for a five-year-
old!

CHARLES WALLACE

2. Defeating IT

As you know, Meg had the only power to save Charles Wallace and, thus, defeat IT! That power is love . . . the love needed to fight HATE, the evil with which IT ruled Camazotz. Help Meg change HATE to LOVE in only five TESSERING moves. You may change only *one* letter with each TESSER, and every time you must make a NEW word!

	H	A	T	E
Tesser #1	__	__	__	__
Tesser #2	__	__	__	__
Tesser #3	__	__	__	__
Tesser #4	__	__	__	__
Tesser #5	__	__	__	__
	L	__	V	E

TWIN SPELL

by JANET LUNN

Illustrated by Emily McCully

I. THE STORY

Jane and Elizabeth were almost drawn to the antique store where they bought the old doll. Afterward nothing was the same. And, when they moved to Aunt Alice's house where the doll "seemed to belong," the twin terrors began. The girls began to have similar dreams and to feel the possession within them of a cruel person long dead. Stranger and stranger occurrences plagued their lives as they sought out the ghostly secret. Then in an explosive climax, the dreaded terror revealed itself.

II. PREREADING DISCUSSION QUESTIONS

The questions which follow are illustrative of the kinds which teachers can prepare for the purpose of releasing children to reveal how they feel *about some of the larger ideas and bigger meanings contained in the book* before it is read by the children.

About Omens and Hunches
1. An *omen* is defined as "any phenomenon supposed to predict good or evil." How many omens can you identify with the specific good or evil event they predicted?
2. A *hunch* is defined as "a premonition or feeling or foreboding of a pleasant or unpleasant future happening." While most of us tend to forget those hunches that never came true, we never seem to forget the *right hunches* we've had! How would you describe the most superfantastic right hunch you've ever had? How did it affect your life?

3. Some people believe very firmly in fortune-tellers, especially after some of the things they predict "really come true." Whether or not you believe in fortune-telling, how can you explain that some predictions of the future do come true?

4. While many people *do not* believe that it's possible to foretell the future, many *do* believe that some people have the gift of ESP (extrasensory perception). How many situations do you know about or which you've been involved in that could be explained *only* as the result of someone's ESP?

About Twins

5. What things do people believe *twins* have that are the *same?* What beliefs do people have about how twins are *different?*

6. How many reasons can you think of that would explain why twins would grow so tired of being twins that they would go to extremes to be "untwins" or unalike? What can you think of that they might do to be dissimilar?

About Family History

7. What are some of the true stories about the very *old family souvenirs* (mementos, treasures, heirlooms) once owned, used, or played with by your grandparents or great-grandparents? (Things such as handmade articles, or toys, or pictures, or jewelry, and so forth.)

8. In your own family history, whom do your parents and grandparents talk about most with pride? Why do they feel this way? Whom do they feel most ashamed of? Why do they feel this way?

III. PREREADING ACTIVITIES

The Prereading Activities which follow purpose to elicit *analogous* or *parallel* experiences from the reader's background so that he/she can identify more intensely with the *feelings* of the

characters in the book—as they interact with other characters, situations, and events—as he/she reads and finds them familiar because they are but one step removed from the real occurrences in his/her life.

Date_____

Name_____

1. **Twin Thoughts**

DOUBLE THOUGHTS

DIRECTIONS: Listed below are some common and-not-so-common ideas which people have about identical twins. Which do you believe are the most ACCURATE statements about TWINS? Put an A on the line in front of those you feel most likely are true. Put an M on the line in front of those which you feel are MYTHS or, simply, old wives' tales—that is, highly improbable.

Most sets of identical twins . . .

_____ 1. are of the same sex.

_____ 2. have one twin that's shy and the other that's oozing with personality.

_____ 3. have one twin who is very orderly and the other who is disorganized.

_____ 4. like the same things.

_____ 5. have one twin that's brighter than the other.

_____ 6. have thoughts and feelings that are closer and stronger than brothers and sisters who are not twins.

_____ 7. sometimes have the same dreams.

_____ 8. occasionally can read each other's minds.

_____ 9. dress alike.

_____10. have one twin that's very cautious; the other takes chances.

2. **Fortune Cards**

TILLIE TAROT TELLS

DIRECTIONS: One year ago today you visited Tillie Tarot's tent at a carnival which was passing through town. After you gave her fifty cents, she asked you to shuffle her FORTUNE CARDS, then she dealt them face up, one at a time, and told you YOUR FORTUNE. Printed on each card below is what she predicted for you ONE YEAR AGO TODAY! On the lines on each of Tillie's cards, write what happened to you this past year that makes you BELIEVE IN TILLIE. How did her predictions about you come true? If one or more didn't come true during the past year, write what you WOULD HAVE LIKED TO HAVE HAPPEN TO YOU.

ROSES CARD

"This card with three ROSES means very good luck will come your way THREE times, but before your good fortune blooms, twice you will feel the thorns of sadness even though your good luck will overcome the pains of discouragement."

_____
_____
_____
_____
_____

ROSES CARD

PIGEON CARD

"This PIGEON card reveals new love entering into your life—the love of a pet for you and you for the pet. Your whole outlook on the people in your world will change for the better as a result."

_____
_____
_____
_____
_____
_____

PIGEON CARD

CAMEO CARD

"This CAMEO card indicates a gift which you will soon receive from someone unexpected—a gift so super, so surprising, that it eclipses any gift or present you've ever received."

_____
_____
_____
_____
_____
_____

CAMEO CARD

DOLL CARD

"This DOLL card predicts either money or a toy—a luxury quite valuable which has been on your mind and in your dreams for a long time, and it will come to you as a result of unexpected good luck at a time when you are most depressed."

_____
_____
_____
_____
_____

DOLL CARD

HOUSE CARD

"When the HOUSE card appears, it signifies a MOVE is in store for you soon—a new home, a new school, a trip which you had no idea was coming."

_____
_____
_____
_____
_____
_____
_____

HOUSE CARD

IV. POSTREADING DISCUSSION QUESTIONS

1. How many reasons can you give that would explain why Jane and Elizabeth often seemed to prefer being "untwins" than twins?

2. How might someone argue that the twins' fight (chap. 5) was caused more by the ways they are *unlike* rather than the strange things they have in common?

3. On page 157, Elizabeth says: *"I wonder if that's what ghosts really are, memories. . . . Leftover memories, left loose because they weren't finished."* As you think about this and other ghost stories you've read, what is your response to Elizabeth's idea?

4. Aunt Alice, and others in the story, simply laughed off those strange and peculiar things that happened by attributing them to *"being just one of those twin things."* What happened in the story that you would refer to as "twin things"?

5. When did the "happenings" stop being *coincidences* and start being part of the Hester mystery for you?

6. The twins were able to connect and solve the mystery of most of the clues almost as fast as they happened, except for one: *Hester's and Amelia's house,* which they searched for unsuccessfully until it was nearly too late! How might you explain why the HOUSE MYSTERY was so difficult to solve?

7. Why would you agree or disagree with the point that although the twins only paid $2.53 for the doll at the "ANTIQUES, DOLLS MENDED" shop, it turned out to be quite a costly purchase in the long run?

8. Why do you think Joe's advice to Jane about *ghosts haunting until they are forgiven* worked in the attic with Hester?

9. Jane and Elizabeth were not the only *pair of doubles* in this story. How can you explain the significance of the various other *twins* which enter into the mystery of the doll?

V. HELPING CHILDREN TO REVEAL
THEIR COMPREHENSION

Name_____

Date_____

1. **If Hester's Shoes Could Talk . . .**

*DIRECTIONS: While locked in the attic, suppose Jane
had found an old pair of Hester's shoes, and while she
was waiting for William to let her out, SHE PUT THEM
ON AND THEY BEGAN TO TALK! What would
Hester have told Jane? How would Hester have explained
the strange happenings? What kinds of "bargains" might
Hester have tried to make? In the ghostly cloud below,
draw what you think could be the most helpful clue
HESTER'S SHOES could give Jane.*

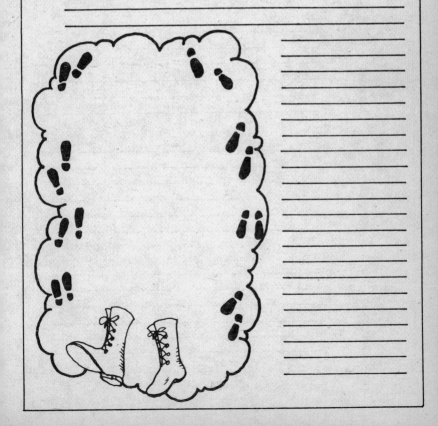

2. Expanding the c**LU**es

DIRECTIONS: As the Private Detective hired by Jane and Elizabeth, you are investigating the eight clues which appear below in your special Private-Eye MAGNIFYING GLASSES. You have now followed up on and completed your investigation of each of the clues and are ready to report back to the twins. Using the lines by each of the clues, expand each one specifically so that Jane and Elizabeth will be able to solve the mystery.

'THE DOLL SHOP'
_____
_____
_____
_____
_____
_____

A HISTORY BOOK
_____
_____
_____
_____
_____
_____

A PIGEON
_____
_____
_____
_____
_____
_____

UNEX-PLAINED MESSES

_____
_____
_____
_____
_____
_____

BROKEN BONES

_____
_____
_____
_____
_____
_____

A MOVE TO A NEW HOUSE

_____
_____
_____
_____
_____
_____

ROSES

_____
_____
_____
_____
_____

A BROOCH

_____
_____
_____
_____
_____
_____

3. **Amelia's Account**

DIRECTIONS: Amelia not only had a doll twin but two different twin owners—about 130 years apart! (Anne and Melissa and Jane and Elizabeth. More than anyone else, AMELIA knows the mysteries of the attic, Hester's ghostly doings, as well as how she came to be in the "ANTIQUES, DOLLS MENDED" shop in the first place. Before going into more natural doll-like behavior and remaining silent forever, Amelia reveals her account of "The Hester Caper." Finish Amelia's story.

My name is Amelia Sabiston, the favorite doll of my owner, Melissa Sabiston. I have a twin, as does Melissa. It is July 22, 1838, the day that my twin's owner, Anne, died . . .

_____

_____

_____

_____

_____

_____

_____

_____

_____

_____

_____

VI. RELATED-TO-READING EXPERIENCES

1. Twin-Spin

Is Hester's ghost doing ghostly things again? Out of thin air she is transmitting an important TWIN-SPELL-PIC-TURE for you! Just follow these directions:

1. Cut out the rectangle below which contains the two magic circles. Paste the rectangle on a piece of cardboard.
2. Neatly cut out both circles or "discs."
3. Cut a piece of string so that it measures about 10 inches.
4. Turn disc #1 over so that the picture part is face down and the cardboard side is up.

Disc #1   Disc #2

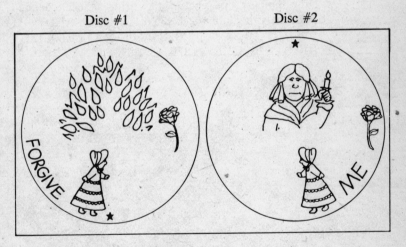

5. Cover the back of disc #1 completely with glue, taking care that the little star is at the bottom (on the underneath side) before you apply the glue.

6. Place the string carefully on the disc with the glue in a precise "east-west" position.

7. Now put the other (unglued) disc on top of the one with the glue (cardboard side against cardboard side), MAKING CERTAIN DISC #2 IS UPSIDE DOWN—that is, the little star at the top of disc #2, before you cut it out, *will now be at the bottom,* exactly opposite the little star on the other side at the bottom of disc #1.

8. Press these until dry to keep them from curling at the edges; also be very careful that they do not slip in any direction.

9. Now, holding one end of the string in each hand, twist the string and watch the disc spin . . . AND . . . WATCH HESTER'S MESSAGE MATERIALIZE RIGHT BEFORE YOUR EYES!

THE WITCH OF BLACKBIRD POND

by

ELIZABETH GEORGE SPEARE

I. THE STORY

Kit Tyler knew, as she gazed for the first time at the cold, bleak shores of Connecticut Colony, that her new home would never be like the shimmering Caribbean Islands she left behind. She was like a tropical bird which has flown to the wrong part of the world. And in the stern, Puritan community of her relatives, she soon felt caged as well, and lonely. In the meadows, the only place where she could feel completely free, she meets another lone and mysterious figure, the old woman known as the Witch of Blackbird Pond. But when their friendship is discovered, Kit is faced with suspicion, fear, and anger. She herself is accused of witchcraft!

II. PREREADING DISCUSSION QUESTIONS

The questions which follow are illustrative of the kinds which teachers can prepare for the purpose of releasing children to reveal how they feel about some of the larger ideas and bigger meanings contained in the book before it is read by the children.

About Attitudes Toward Strangers
1. What kinds of things have been said about or done to new students in your school who *dressed* or *acted* or *spoke* so differently that it was difficult for them to fit in?

91

2. When people from foreign countries or from certain places in the United States come to live in a new community, they often bring with them certain habits, customs, and mannerisms that were "normal" and acceptable in their old communities but now are out of place and even offensive to some people. What are some of these which you have observed *turn a lot of people off?*

3. How many different reasons can you think of that would explain why we are sometimes afraid of people who look or act in a different way?

4. Frequently, we give people *labels* to describe some peculiarity they have—whether it's physical, or manner of dress, or behavior. Hannah *Hippie,* Sammy *Straight, Prissy* Pauline, Nancy *Knows-It-All, Crackpot* Cranston, and Wanda *Wishy-Washy* are a few examples of such labels not often used in a friendly way. How do you feel such labels affect the way others think of those people given the labels? How are such labels harmful? How could they be helpful?

5. What reactions do you believe would result if a young man dressed in dirty jeans, shoulder-length hair, barefoot, large dark glasses, and a skull and bones painted on the back of a torn shirt offered a *free* service of carrying heavy bags of groceries from your local supermarket check-out counter to the customer's car? Why do you think people would or would not accept this free service?

About Uniformity

6. In many families, the children are given no choice but to follow their parents' religion. Why do you suppose this occurs? What advantages or disadvantages can you think of that would explain such practices?

7. In some schools in this country, and in many schools abroad, everyone must dress the same. Why do you

suppose such rules exist? How would you feel if you had to attend such a school?

8. Seasonal festivals and celebrations of certain holidays are very popular traditions that could be called mass exercises in *uniformity,* such as (a) the sending of Christmas cards, (b) family dinners at Thanksgiving, (c) parties and resolutions made at New Year's, (d) masquerades on Halloween, (e) picnics and fireworks on the Fourth of July, (f) parades and speeches on Memorial Day, and so on. What causes a person to take part in such activities *even though he/she doesn't want to?* How would you describe the feelings a person could have if he/she doesn't participate in such celebrations when everyone else around him/her does?

III. PREREADING ACTIVITIES

The Prereading Activities which follow purpose to elicit *analogous* or *parallel* experiences from the reader's background so that he/she can identify more intensely with the *feelings* of the characters in the book—as they interact with other characters, situations, and events—as he/she reads and finds them familiar because they are but one step removed from the real occurrences in his/her daily life.

1. Personality Give-a-Ways

DIRECTIONS: Suppose that, of six people whom you consider your very best friends, each has three OUT-STANDING character or personality traits listed below and that it is possible for each to GIVE AWAY one trait! *In doing so, however, each one will have the remaining two for the rest of his/her life. For each of your friends, tell which TRAIT you would want him/her to give away and how you think your friend could manage to have a happy and successful life with the remaining two.*

FRIEND ONE: (1) a compulsive liar, (2) has great beauty, (3) has an unpleasant body odor (Give-A-Way: _____)

_____

_____

FRIEND TWO: (1) very intelligent, (2) terribly conceited, (3) has a pimpled face (Give-A-Way: ___)

_____

_____

FRIEND THREE: (1) confined to a wheelchair, (2) a life-long, expensive, fashionable wardrobe, (3) rude and cruel (Give-A-Way: _____)

_____

_____

FRIEND FOUR: (1) an honor student, (2) excessive pride, (3) anti-women's lib (Give-A-Way: ___)

_____

_____

FRIEND FIVE: (1) swears profanely, (2) an apple-polisher, (3) extra-ordinarily creative (Give-A-Way: _____)

_____

_____

FRIEND SIX: (1) a braggart, (2) a bully, (3) a born leader (Give-A-Way: _____)

_____

_____

2.   **Wisdom or Witchcraft?**
In Colonial times, the following things were very popular. Find out what you can about each and, in your own words, write a simple definition that would explain what each one means. Then, under each, indicate whether you would be FOR or AGAINST such things if they existed today.

THE HORNBOOK

☐ For ☐ Against

THE OL' DELUDER-SATAN LAW (Massachusetts)

☐ For ☐ Against

THE STOCKS

☐ For ☐ Against

DAMES SCHOOLS

☐ For ☐ Against

IV. POSTREADING DISCUSSION QUESTIONS

1. In what ways do you think Kit *cast a spell* on the children she taught?

2. If Kit's grandfather could give her advice, what might he tell her about *teaching?*

3. The author does not tell you why William did not appear when Kit was in the shed or as a defendant at the pretrial. What reasons can you give which might explain his apparent "uncaring" behavior?

4. What do you think Kit found most difficult about her new life?

5. Why do you think Goodwife Cruff, as well as several others in Wethersfield, *wanted* to believe that Hannah and Kit were witches and punish them?

6. What is your opinion of how the Puritans think about (1) religion, (2) the home, (3) school, (4) punishments, and (5) girls? What are some similar beliefs we hold today? What are some of today's beliefs that certain groups are trying to change?

7. What do you think Hannah Tupper's *real magic* was?

8. How do you interpret Hannah's statement to Kit when she said:

   "But remember, thee has never escaped at all if love is not there."? (P. 170.)

9. Why do you think Kit strongly resisted her impulse to tell Mercy that John loved her? Even when she thought John might never return, why do you think Kit still kept the secret?

10. Hannah Tupper (p. 97) said to Kit: *"The answer is in thy heart. . . . Thee can always hear it if thee listens for it."* What do you think she meant? In what ways did Kit follow her advice?

V. HELPING CHILDREN REVEAL
THEIR COMPREHENSION

1.

```
□□ □□□ □□□□ □□□□□□□□
WETHERSFIELD
□□□□ □□□□□□□□□ □□□□
COMPUTER MATING
□□□ □□□□□□ □□ □□□□□
SERVICE,INC.
□□□□□ □□□□□□□ □□□□□□□□
```

Name_____

Date_____

DIRECTIONS: You are running the Wethersfield Computer Mating Service. Each young person in the story has submitted to you a brief biographical sketch and also indicates what he/she is looking for in a mate. As an expert in such matters, you then are to choose a mate for each—agreeing or disagreeing with the author, if you wish. Be sure to give a brief statement which explains your reason for each match.

Name of Client	Biographical Sketch	Mated with	Reason
TYLER, KIT			
WOOD, MERCY			
WOOD, JUDITH			
HOLBROOK, JOHN			
EATON, NAT			
ASHBY, WILLIAM			

2. **Crimes of the Times**

DIRECTIONS: Listed below are various "CRIMES" which were committed by various people in this book in the late 1600s. Some of the "CRIMES" broke local Wethersfield Civil Laws, while others broke Connecticut Colony laws. Some "CRIMES" were simply against the unwritten MORAL Ways, Codes, and Beliefs of the majority of the citizens and could not be punished by trial in a court of law. Still others violated the superstitious fears the townsfolk had because they believed the Devil walked the earth and could bewitch men, women, and children.

Help sort out the crimes for what they really were then! If they broke Wethersfield or Connecticut Colony Law, list them under the "Jail Door." If they broke local Moral and Religious Rules and Ways of Living, put them under the "Puritan Hat." And, if they were considered matters of Witchcraft, then place them under the "Fortune-Teller's Ball."

After you finish, what names can you associate with each of the "CRIMES"?

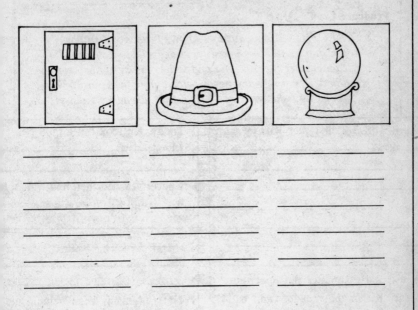

_____   _____   _____

_____   _____   _____

_____   _____   _____

_____   _____   _____

_____   _____   _____

_____   _____   _____

LIST OF CRIMES OF THE TIMES

1. Not going to Meeting
2. Celebrating Halloween
3. A girl who can swim
4. Disobeying parents
5. Following Quaker beliefs
6. Slander and libel
7. Having a cat for a pet
8. Dressing in fancy clothes
9. Playing games
10. A child's not learning to read and write
11. Loyalty to the King of England
12. Dramatizing the Bible
13. Reading books of fiction
14. Making jack-o'-lanterns

3. **Prudence Cruff's DIARY**

DIRECTIONS: As you now know, Prudence Cruff was not a dumb, feeble-minded, retarded child. As soon as Kit taught her how to read and write, she began to keep a diary. Her first entry began with a date in April 1687 . . . the day she first met Kit. Fill in Prudence's diary!

April 1687: I first met Kit Tyler
when_____

_____

_____

and I felt_____

_____

                                P.C.

It was early summer the next time
I saw Kit in the meadow and we_

_____

_____

At first, I felt_____

but then_____

_____

                                P.C.

The most wonderful thing began to
happen today when Kit took me to
Hannah Tupper's house and_____

_____

_____

_____

_____

                                P.C.

Today, Kit took out a quill pen
and_____

I never realized then how valuable
that would be later on when_____

_____

_____

_____

                                P.C.

Nat Eaton has been helping me
at Hannah's house when Kit can'
get away. I think that Kit, Nat, and
Hannah are just about_____

_____

_____

                                P.C.

The most horrible thing almost
happened today! I'm so glad tha
Nat came to get me. Not only did
we_____

_____

but, also, I know my life with m
parents will be_____

                                P.C

VI. RELATED-TO-READING EXPERIENCES

1. Write a sermon for Dr. Gershom Bulkeley telling the Colonists why they must be loyal to the king.
2. Find out all you can about a hornbook and make an exact replica of one.
3. Nearly all the Colonists were superstitious and had faith in signs, charms, and omens. They believed in witches and in witchcraft and were afraid.
    (a) Find and read the poem "Cotton Mather" by Rosemary and Stephen Vincent Benét. Find out about Reverend Cotton Mather and the Salem witch trials.
    (b) Write the script for a trial in which Hannah Tupper is tried for witchcraft. Include Cotton Mather as one of the witnesses against her.
4. Paint a picture of how you believe the meadow must have looked before Hannah's house was destroyed.
5. The Charter of 1662 granted by King Charles II of England to Connecticut included the Fundamental Orders which declared that all powers of government should come from the people, there should be no taxation without representation, and that all loyal citizens could vote. Find out about charters granted to other colonies and about the self-government of each colony. Write a paper which states your position on why the Colonists, though most were Englishmen, would want to fight against England to keep their own laws.

THE ACTIVE-ENZYME LEMON-FRESHENED JUNIOR HIGH SCHOOL WITCH

by E. W. HILDICK

Illustrated by Iris Schweitzer

I. THE STORY

"I first discovered I was a Witch with Power to Conjure Up the Dead when I was but twelve that time (last month) on vacation up in West Salem. It was not THE Salem up in Massachusetts; it was one of the Salems up near the New York–Connecticut border. But borders are powerfully Magic Places and the Witchcraft was real enough. . . ."

So writes Alison McNair—alias Ariadne—in her Witch's Workbook. From the moment Alison, a redheaded, incorrigible, exasperating, yet somehow lovable fury, opens the pages of *How to Be a Witch* and reads of the unusual powers of redhaired witches, she knows that sorcery is her natural calling. And with her sister Jeannie, alias Jezebel, as a sorceress's apprentice, they begin in earnest to dabble in the occult, producing some strange and unforeseen results.

II. PREREADING DISCUSSION QUESTIONS

The questions which follow are illustrative of the kinds which teachers can prepare for the purpose of releasing children to reveal how they feel about some of the larger ideas and bigger meanings contained in the book before it is read by children.

About Put-ons and Put-downs

1. What would you do and/or say to a person to convince him/her that you were *sincerely sorry and apologetic* when, actually, you REALLY WERE NOT?
2. How might you try to make an angry teacher feel sorry for you?
3. What specific examples can you give that would show why you believe or don't believe that when a person is put down in front of others it makes him/her worse instead of teaching a lesson?
4. What situations would you approve of in which a person put on a phony act to hide his/her real feelings?

About Being Patient

5. How can you explain why it's so difficult, if possible at all, to get a young child to be patient when he/she is about to get or do something very exciting?
6. How would you describe an example of a time when you did something on *impulse* and it turned out well? How would you describe an example of another time when you decided on *impulse* to do something and it was a disaster?

About Unusual, Super Powers

7. When a young person encounters a whole string of bad luck, it is easy to believe that he/she is being punished by some strange, evil, magical thing or power. What do people try to do to *turn their bad luck around?*
8. At one time or other, everyone has had something *uncanny* occur which the person already knew about or else, knew was going to happen! When this takes place, we often say, *"It must be ESP!"* How would you describe a happening in which you were convinced that you must have had some kind of ESP (extrasensory perception).
9. How would you describe a situation when you found yourself *concentrating* on a person so strongly that it caused him/her to do *exactly what you wanted him/her to do?*

III. PREREADING ACTIVITIES

The Prereading Activities which follow purpose to elicit *analogous* or *parallel* experiences from the reader's background so that he/she can identify more intensely with the *feelings* of the

---

Name_____

Date_____

1. **Your Personal Inventory of Hexes—Whammies and Spells**

> *DIRECTIONS: Below are a number of circumstances which some people feel* THEY HAVE CAUSED BY INVOKING SOME MAGICAL POWER *through some sort of special chant, jinx, prayer, ESP, strong wish, or superstitious bad/good luck charm. Put your own special witch or warlock mark on the blanks in front of each item below which you feel* YOU CAUSED *or at least should get* SOME CREDIT FOR CAUSING TO HAPPEN *through some inexplicable* HEX, WHAMMY, *or* SPELL!

_____1. An important, scheduled test in school, which you were sure to fail, was called off!

_____2. Your team is ahead by only one point and, with thirty seconds to go in the game, the visiting team tries one final super play . . . and misses!

_____3. You've spent your allowance, blew your savings, and borrowed all you can from friends when the most mar-

---

characters in the book—as they interact with other characters, situations, and events—as he/she reads and finds them familiar because they are but one step removed from the real occurrences in his/her life.

velous bargain in your life comes your way: *a garage sale in which there's a practically new stereo system and a fantastic record collection priced at thirty-five dollars.* On the way home from school you turn your ankle and fall. There in the gutter you find a fifty-dollar bill!

_____4. You're late to catch a bus or train, and as you rush to get there on time, you hope and pray that, for once, it's a couple of minutes late so you can make it. It is. You do!

_____5. To get out of a tough situation or an unfair and difficult job, you hope to get sick enough to be excused. And it happens!

_____6. You are liked by almost everyone, but you've never been really popular or well-known or what one might call a winner. You find yourself in an election in which you want more than anything else to win. And you do!

_____7. You've never won anything in your life even though you've always bought tickets and chances on a lot of things, just to support the charity or cause. But this time you buy a twenty-five-cent chance on something too unbelievable ever to dream you could have. Your ticket wins!

_____8. You have a fear and strong dislike for someone—so much so that you hope something very unpleasant happens to teach him/her a good lesson. It does!

Name_____

Date_____

2. **An Occult Scavenger Hunt**

DIRECTIONS: Below is a list of NECESSARY items or tools for beginning witches and warlocks. It is NOT by chance that there are 13 items; or that one must only begin to collect them at 1300 hours (1:00 P.M.) on ANY 13th day (multiples of thirteen) starting with the hour of 13:13 (1:13 P.M.) on October 31 (November 12 and 24, December 6, 18, 30, and so forth); or that you are permitted only 13 minutes PER ITEM—a total of 169 minutes (or 2 hours and 49 minutes). These are magical musts! If you are ready to begin your apprenticeship, you'll need to do some preplanning before one of the bewitching hours mentioned above comes your way so that you will lose no time on your 13-minute per 13-item scavenger hunt. All items should be unwanted or discarded. While waiting for the right hour of the right day, you may want to do some pre-searching and jot down the locations of magic tools.

NOTE: Three substitutes may be made if they are in the "spirit" of the requirements on the list and one feels "right" about making the substitution.

OCCULT ITEMS	LOCATIONS
1. 1 small table, top no larger than 26 inches X 26 inches.	
2. 13 different spices/herbs (one of these must be 13 tablespoons of salt; ½ teaspoon of the other twelve is sufficient), each labeled correctly in a plain envelope.	
3. 1 bracelet.	
4. 1 necklace with 13 objects.	
5. 1 ring.	
6. 1 31 inch X 31 inch piece of green, blue, or black cloth.	
7. 1 small flashlight, covered with blue cellophane, that can be switched on and stood on end.	
8. 1 girdle cord: a piece of rope 182 inches long with knots tied 13 inches apart.	
9. 1 penknife (pocket knife).	
10. 1 green-ink ball-point pen.	
11. 1 workbook (notebook with plain cover, and unlined pages for drawing and writing).	
12. 1 tiny bell attached to 13-inch piece of black ribbon to be worn on wrist or ankle.	
13. 13 assorted jars and small bottles, empty but clean, and all with screw caps. (One must be a goblet, another a chafing dish—no lids, caps, tops necessary.)	

IV. POSTREADING DISCUSSION QUESTIONS

1. When Jeannie-*Jezebel* looked into the Magic Mirror, she saw, among other things, two red-colored snakes fighting, a burning tower sticking out of the side of a mountain and in which someone is trapped, a speckled bird with a red and gold tongue, and two midgets fighting in a covered dish. Alison-*Ariadne* believed her sister since she knew that her sister was NOT a kidder. Why were or were you not surprised to find that none of Jeannie-*Jezebel*'s visions came true?
2. Why do you think Mr. McNair acted the way he did when he caught his two daughters practicing witchcraft?
3. Why do you think some readers of this book would argue that Alison-*Ariadne Atropos Arachne* really WASN'T all that serious about becoming a witch?
4. If you had to come up with two or three examples of magical happenings which *could have resulted* from Alison McNair's dabbling in witchcraft, what would they be?

5. If Emmeline, Alison's best friend, had doubted Alison-*Ariadne*'s abilities in casting spells and succeeding in other magical feats, what do you think Alison would have said to convince Emmeline she was wrong?

6. In the story, you get several clear examples of Alison's talents to *"hustle"* other people. What do you think someone might mean if he/she said, *"Sure she hustles others, but Alison McNair—alias Ariadne-the-witch—hustles HERSELF more than anyone else!"*?

7. What things do you think could have been said to Alison that *might have convinced* her that she WASN'T under a Magical Attack?

V. HELPING CHILDREN REVEAL
THEIR COMPREHENSION

Name_____

Date_____

1. **One Thing Leads to Another!**

DIRECTIONS: The author gives a specific example of an Alison "One-Thing-Leads-to-Another-Thing" (p. 12) when he explains Alison's discovery of her Witch Powers as a result of beginning the summer vacation with the MEASLES:

A BUG + A COUGH + A SNIFFLE + A HEAD-ACHE + A FEVER + A SWEAT + A RASH = THE MEASLES.

Below are the BEGINNINGS and the ENDS of several other Alison "Happenings," and they need your addition of each THING which you believe LEADS TO THE OTHER. As you can see from the sample, there are many possibilities and no "right" solutions except for those that you remember which make sense to you.

HAPPENING #1

_____

(A Sample)

1. MEASLES

2. *Sylvie*

_____

3. *Punishment*

_____

4. *The Book of Magic*

_____

5. *Mother Misses a Putt*

_____

6. *Bedtime Stories*

_____

7. Alison-the-Witch

HAPPENING #2

1. The Old Summer House

2. _____

3. _____

4. _____

5. _____

6. _____

7. Norton the Second

HAPPENING #3

1. Counteracting the Fetch

2. _____

3. _____

4. _____

5. _____

6. _____

7. Angie-Ariadne the First

HAPPENING #4

1. Equipping the Tower

2. _____

3. _____

4. _____

5. _____

6. _____

7. Jezebel: the Start of a Coven

HAPPENING #5

1. Magic in the Tower

2. _____

3. _____

4. _____

5. _____

6. _____

7. The Raising of Mr. McNair

2. **Matching Ariadne's Moods**

> *DIRECTIONS: As you know, Alison McNair practices for hours to make her MOOD FACES believable. As you can see below, Alison is pictured in each of the five moods she used in the story: GOOD, HURT, CALM, PA-TIENT and UNEASY. On the blank in front of each of the statements about a situation in the story, match the Alison-Ariadne face which you feel she would have used by putting a G for Good, H for Hurt, C for Calm, P for Patient, and U for Uneasy.*

GOOD   HURT   CALM   PATIENT   UNEASY

_____ 1. Mr. McNair surprises Alison and Jeannie in the tower during their "Raising the Devil" ceremony.

_____ 2. Alison solves the problem of getting the altar table from the basement like a mathematical equation.

_____ 3. Mr. Crowther almost catches Alison in the tool shed.

_____ 4. Alison's TV show starring Sylvie, Jeannie's doll, fails due to an unappreciative audience.

_____ 5. Alison effectively arranged the "Potent Defenses" she obtained to ward off the Magical Attack.

_____ 6. Alison awakes from a nightmare and sees the Fetch climbing the apartment house wall across the court.

_____ 7. Alison's bottle of bent pins stopped a thief, not a Fetch.

_____ 8. Alison's parents laughed and teased her about playing witch.

_____ 9. A book on witchcraft discovers Alison and she discovers that red-haired witches are the most powerful.

_____10. Alison is trapped in a lie in the lair after her vision comes true in an all-too-human bathroom.

3. **Dewitching Ariadne's Spells, Hexes, and Wizardry**

DIRECTIONS: As a Sorcerer or Sorceress with Powers 100 percent stronger than Ariadne Atropos Arachne's, you are now able to DE-WITCH her and explain away all her doings in very UNMAGIC terms! All you need to do is to say Alison McNair's witch name BACKWARD three times and then begin to write explanations for each of the items below. Ready . . .

Arachne Atropos Ariadne
Arachne Atropos Ariadne
Arachne Atropos Ariadne

DEWITCH #1: Alison finds the book on witchcraft:

_____

_____

DEWITCH #2: Mrs. McNair misses a five-inch putt:

_____

_____

114

DEWITCH #3: The favorable predictions of the Magic Pendulum:_____

_____

_____

DEWITCH #4: Jeannie's visions in the Magic Mirror:

_____

_____

DEWITCH #5: The reincarnation of Norton II at the Dumb Supper:_____

_____

_____

DEWITCH #6: Alison's twenty omens to prove the Magical Attack:_____

_____

_____

DEWITCH #7: The Fetch Alison saw in the night:

_____

_____

DEWITCH #8: The effectiveness of Alison's Potent Defenses against a Magical Attack:

_____

_____

Name_____

Date_____

1. Investigation #1
By Alison McNair
TOPFLIGHT FULLY AUTOMATED JUNIOR
HIGH SCHOOL GIRL DETECTIVE

> *DIRECTIONS: As Alison says farewell to Ariadne and all her witching tools and assumes a new goal of becoming a Lady Detective like Angie Morrison, she remembers the disturbingly real VISIONS which Jeannie-Jezebel revealed as she gazed into the black plate in the tower. Therefore she decides the best way to work out her Private-Eye Apprenticeship is to find the MEANINGS IN JEANNIE'S VISIONS. After listing the clues, she begins her first case and, in typical Alison fashion, COMPLETES IT SUCCESSFULLY. As her trustworthy Assistant, you file this Official Report on Investigation #1:*

THE CLUES:
1. A snow-covered valley with two dark pools
2. Two fighting, red-colored snakes
3. A fire in the top of a tower on a mountain
4. A person trapped in the tower
5. Long table set with white dishes with covers
6. Brownies, stew, and two fighting midgets
7. Speckled bird with red and gold tongue
8. A black cat jumping at a black bird

2.   Toad, Load, CODE—Smells, Dwells, SPELLS!

As you know, in her letters to Emmeline, Alison used her own special code to keep prying people from reading their mail. She used combinations of homonyms, synonyms, and antonyms (see pp. 128-132) to do the job—like the title of this which is really CODE-SPELLS. Below you will find the mysterious and magical spellings of words by superintelligent Wilhelm Warlock. To match his tremendous powers you need to solve thirteen of them. For each one over thirteen, you're one Hex Step closer to becoming a GRADUATE WARLOCK (or WITCH), which means you've solved all twenty correctly spelled!

MAGIC CODE	HUMAN SPELLING	HEX HINT
1 B		An insect
2. ME		TV Awards
3. IC		Frozen streets
4. NME		Opposite of friend
5. T		A drink
6. C		A body of water
7. IV		A vine
8. MT		Not a drop left
9. P		A vegetable
10. NRG		Vim and vigor
11. AT		A number: LXXX

MAGIC CODE	HUMAN SPELLING	HEX HINT
12. EZ		Not hard
13. VU		Scene from a mountaintop
14. DK		Toothpaste prevents this
15. KG		Very clever
16. XL		The best
17. IL		In theaters and churches
18. SA		Written composition
19. XS		Too much
20. NV		Jealous

3. Stepping Through the Page of Wanda Witch's Notebook

Only Wanda Witch and you, her trained Assistant, can step THROUGH the very small black page at the end of her notebook, and PULL IT OVER your entire body —all the way over your head! The size of the black page in Wanda's notebook is 7 inches X 5 inches! Follow the steps below. When you finish, place it on the floor, open it up, spread it apart, step into the "Witch's Circle" it forms, then pull it up over your body, cackling all the while.

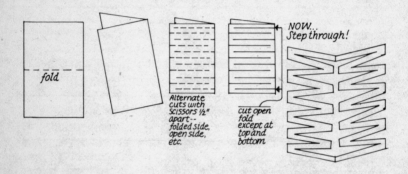

fold

Alternate cuts with scissors ½" apart-- folded side, open side, etc.

cut open fold except at top and bottom

NOW... Step through!

THE GHOST IN THE NOONDAY SUN

by SID FLEISCHMAN

Illustrated by Warren Chappell

I. THE STORY

Legend has it that a person born at the stroke of midnight can see ghosts. And Oliver Finch was born at the stroke of midnight. Since Captain Scratch believes in both legends and ghosts, he kidnaps young Oliver and makes him a captive on the *Bloody Hand*. Oliver's job is to find the ghost of Gentleman Jack, who is supposed to be dancing on the treasure that Scratch and his pirates buried many years before. With his life hanging on the success of the ghost hunt, Oliver determines to escape. He is a resourceful captive, but things go badly. For example, when he drops a ballast stone on the head of one of the pirates, it only bounces off. Nevertheless, with the help of another pirate named Jack o' Lantern, he hatches an ingenious plot that leads to both treasure and rescue.

II. PREREADING DISCUSSION QUESTIONS

The questions which follow are illustrative of the kinds which teachers can prepare for the purpose of releasing children to reveal how they feel *about some of the larger ideas and bigger meanings contained in the book* before it is read by the children.

About Ghosts, Visions, and Other Preternatural Beings
    1. Why do you suppose even the toughest, bravest person you know can become nervous and frightened in the attic of a deserted house, during a severe thunderstorm,

when he/she sees unusual shadows and hears strange sounds?

2. How can you explain why so many people are willing to go to, pay, and believe in *spiritualists* who claim they can contact the deceased in the other world?

3. Most everyone knows about some of the most common *superstitions* many people have, such as broken mirrors, black cats, walking under a ladder, and so forth. What kinds of *superstitions* do you know about which are associated with death and dying?

4. How might you explain the fact that so many *nonsuperstitious* people get more than a little nervous when alone at night in a cemetery?

About Compulsion and Greed

5. How would you make a distinction between someone who is *greedy* and someone who has everything but wastes nothing and spends nothing except for absolute necessities?

6. How would you describe what things you have felt *compelled* to do—no one made you do them but, rather, YOU FELT YOU JUST HAD TO DO them whether or not they made any sense?

7. Some people are identified as *compulsive* eaters, others as *compulsive* talkers; still others as *compulsive* spenders, television watchers, cardplayers, and thieves, for example. How many arguments *for* and *against* COMPULSIVENESS can you give?

8. What could cause someone to think that a person who is *very thrifty* is also *greedy?*

About Kidnapping and Stealing

9. When people steal things, they are called thieves, but when they steal human beings, they are called *kidnappers*. Whether thieves or kidnappers, usually the reason for these criminal acts is *money*. What are other different reasons for someone's kidnapping another human being? For kidnapping animals?

III. PREREADING ACTIVITIES

The Prereading Activities which follow purpose to elicit *analogous* or *parallel* experiences from the reader's background so that he/she can identify more intensely with the *feelings* of the characters in the book—as they interact with other characters, situations, and events—as he/she reads and finds them familiar because they are but one step removed from the real occurrences in his/her life.

What's in a Name?

Suppose you have just won a free round-the-world trip by sea and that you can pick YOUR SHIP as well as your CAPTAIN and CREW from the names below. Which SHIP sounds best to you? Which CAPTAIN? Which FIRST MATE? Which SECOND MATE? Which BOSUN?

SHIPS' NAMES	CAPTAINS' NAMES	CREWS' NAMES
The Bloody Hand	Captain Walk de Plank	Stretch M. Bones
The Sweet Molly	Captain Harry Scratch	Cannibal Fiji
The Leaky Tub	Captain Ghostly Ghoul	Jack o' Lantern
The Monsters' Rage	Captain Juda Revenge	Paws Jibboom
The Dredgie	Captain Angel D'Evil	Gentleman Jack
Doomed		Heeza Nutz
		John Ringrose
		Tuffas Poison

SHIP'S NAME_____

CAPTAIN'S NAME_____

FIRST MATE_____

SECOND MATE_____

BOSUN_____

2. Prisoners' Aid

The following people have all been taken prisoner. The only things they have are: (a) an empty shoebox, (b) a green wax candle, (c) a spool of thread, (d) a pocket knife, (e) plastic bag, (f) a coat hanger, (g) a pair of sunglasses, and (h) ESP (extrasensory perception). Since YOU are a RESCUE ADVICE EXPERT and also have unusual ESP POWERS, your job, should you choose to accept it, IS TO USE YOUR ESP AND SUGGEST A PLAN FOR RESCUE TO THE FOLLOWING PRISONERS:

RESCUE PLAN

Shirley Shanghaied

Locked in a cabin, three days at sea.

Harold Hightower

Locked in a small office on the fortieth floor of a skyscraper.

Roberta Ransome

Locked in a tiny mountain cabin in Tennessee.

Charley Cashe

Locked in a cellar of a deserted farm-house.

IV. POSTREADING DISCUSSION QUESTIONS

1. On page 4, Oliver Finch notices what he describes as a *"scurvy-looking ship"* anchored in Nantucket harbor by the name of *Sweet Molly*. Since it was so scarred and tattered, he thought it seemed *"a contrary name for such a beggarly ship."* How can you now explain why Oliver's first impressions were or were not justified?

2. For his twelfth birthday, Oliver Finch received a jackknife, a gold Spanish doubloon, and some fruit tarts. Why do you think these presents did or didn't bring a lot of happiness to Oliver?

3. Suppose Captain Scratch *could* read! How do you think he might have acted if he had been able to read Oliver's sign:

    "Help. Am prisoner aboard Sweet Molly.
    On southerly course from Nantucket."

4. How would you think it might be possible to argue that Captain Scratch's beliefs in and fears of dredgies and ghosts are a result of his guilty conscience?

5. Not only was the first mate's name (John Ringrose) different from all the other men on the *Bloody Hand,* but, also, his actions. What reasons, therefore, can you give that would explain why he ever became part of the crew on a pirate ship under the evil command of such a man as Captain Scratch?

6. As the *Bloody Hand* was sinking, Jack o' Lantern made a choice between the gold and water and bananas! Why did or didn't you find this surprising and unexpected behavior for him?

7. What guesses can you make that could explain why Jack o' Lantern decided to convince the *live* Captain Scratch that he was nothing more than a *ghost* of the *dead* Harry Scratch?

8. Oliver Finch and Jibboom, almost from the very beginning of the story, seemed not to be the best of friends at all! What opinions do you have about the situation which de-

veloped in which Oliver gave himself up to Captain Scratch and almost certain death in order to save the life of Jibboom?

9. What example of *cleverness* and *bravery* impressed you most about Oliver Finch? What's an example of Oliver's *stupidity* that amazed you the most?

10. Why do you suppose Oliver had so much difficulty in trying to decide whether or not to believe in dredgies, ghosts, and the legend of the powers that one has if he/she is born on the stroke of midnight?

V. HELPING CHILDREN TO REVEAL THEIR COMPREHENSION

Name_____

Date_____

1. **Pieces o' Gold**

DIRECTIONS: As you know, thanks to Oliver Finch's cleverness, the gold was found, but lost again perhaps forever, as a result of the decision which had to be made: food and water vs. the gold! As young as he was, it was hard for Oliver NOT to grab a few PIECES O' GOLD and stuff them in his pocket as a souvenir of his year-long adventure. There were seven in all and, during the two months it took him to get home after being rescued by a turtle boat, he scratched a few words on each with his jackknife so he wouldn't forget anything important when his father asked, as he knew he would, "Where is it thee has been, son?" Oliver's PIECES O' GOLD are opposite. What adventure can you tell with each?

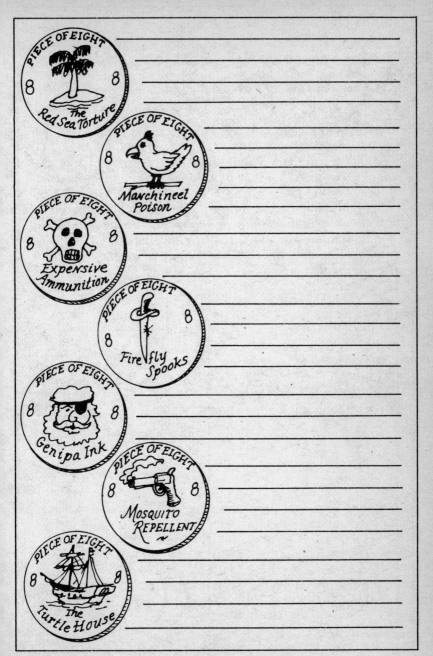

PIECE OF EIGHT — 8 8
The Red Sea Torture

PIECE OF EIGHT — 8 8
Manchineel Poison

PIECE OF EIGHT — 8 8
Expensive Ammunition

PIECE OF EIGHT — 8 8
Firefly Spooks

PIECE OF EIGHT — 8 8
Genipa Ink

PIECE OF EIGHT — 8 8
Mosquito Repellent

PIECE OF EIGHT — 8 8
The Turtle House

2.

DIRECTIONS: The author has commissioned you, the president of the BETTE C. ROSS FLAG-MAKING CO., to make PERSONALIZED flags for each of the characters from the story listed below—at a thousand dollars per flag. Each of your CHARACTER-istic FLAGS is to have the following FOUR things on it which unmistakably symbolize the person for whom it was made: (1) COLOR, (2) DESIGN, (3) INSIGNIA, and (4) SLOGAN. You agree to take on the job and start to work!

CAPTAIN
HARRY SCRATCH

JOHN RINGROSE

CANNIBAL

HAJJI

JACK O' LANTERN

BILLY BOMBAY

Plaguey Duberous Number 13

Name_____

Date_____

DIRECTIONS: *After being marooned on Gentleman Jim's island for all his murderous evil, Captain Harry Scratch begins to ponder about how all the bad luck could have happened to him so quickly. Then, superstitious as he is, he remembers about Jack o' Lantern and how he left him to die as a castaway because there were THIRTEEN men aboard the BLOODY HAND. Suddenly he realizes that he HADN'T SUCCEEDED in reducing his numbers to twelve but that he had THIRTEEN all along. Old plaguey, duberous number 13 had caused all his "misluck"! Quickly he squeezes out the juice from thirteen genipas, tears off his shirt, and (since he doesn't know about the disappearing "ink") begins to record the awful events he BLAMES ON THIS THIRTEEN FOUL-UP!*

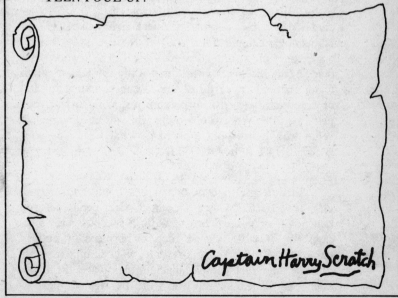

Captain Harry Scratch

VI. RELATED-TO-READING EXPERIENCES

1. **Ship Ahoy!**

   What can you learn about the special vocabulary or language used aboard ships? What can you uncover about the time-telling system of bells? What can you find out about the meanings of flags and flag signals used aboard ships? Just as people driving automobiles have the right of way in certain instances, so, too, do boats and ships have to follow the right-of-way laws. What can you learn about such rules?

   Once you have dug up this NAUTICAL TREASURE from the deep, prepare an interesting display of your information for others to enjoy as well as learn from.

2. **Blueprint for Ghosting**

   Suppose you were asked to be in charge of the GHOST ROOM at your school carnival and you wanted to make it *really* spectacular! In addition to normal supplies you would need (such as tables, sheets, paper, and so forth), you have available for your use (1) a tape recorder, (2) a black light and black light paints, (3) an 8mm movie camera, film, and projector, and (4) a slide projector. You plan to convince EVERYONE who enters that he/she can *see and talk with* Billy the Kid, Captain Kidd, Belle Starr, or any other famous criminal, pirate, or desperado you wish to prepare for. What would your plans be like? What preparation will you need to make? What would the room look like? What would be your BLUEPRINT FOR GHOSTING?

3. **Writing Coded Messages with (artificial) Genipa**

   Squeeze a lemon or two into a bottle and mark it GENIPA JUICE. Using a pointed stick, penholder and pen point, or a small brush, write a special secret message—or draw a treasure map on a piece of *unlined* paper. Let your "ink" dry. (It will disappear more quickly than real genipa juice!) Then place the paper *near* a hot light bulb and watch the message reappear.

THE GREAT BRAIN

by JOHN D. FITZGERALD

Illustrated by Mercer Mayer

I. THE STORY

The Great Brain is Tom D. Fitzgerald, aged ten. The story is
told by J.D., a sometimes confounded but always admiring
younger brother. Such people as Mr. Standish, the mean school-
master, regret the day they came up against The Great Brain.
But others, like the Jensen kids lost in Skeleton Cave; Basil,
the Greek kid; or Andy, who lost his leg and his friends, know
that Tom's Great Brain never fails.

II. PREREADING DISCUSSION QUESTIONS

*The questions which follow are illustrative of the kinds which
teachers can prepare for the purpose of releasing children to
reveal how* they feel *about some of the larger ideas and bigger
meanings contained in the book* before it is read by the children.

About Being Mercenary
1. What opinions do you have about people who won't
   do anything for anyone unless they get money for it?
2. What feelings do you know your classmates have
   about the few who are always the big spenders—that
   is, those who always seem to have a lot of money to
   throw around and use it to get almost anything they
   want?
3. At one time or other you've probably heard someone
   say: *"He's too busy worshiping the almighty dollar to
   care about anyone or anything else!"* How would you
   describe this kind of person?

About Reputations

4. Sometimes a person gets a reputation for *being clever,* or *brave,* or *smart,* or *honest* quite by accident—or by "being lucky." Then, usually, he/she finds he/she has to try hard *to live up to it.* What kinds of things would make such a person feel he has to live up to his reputation? What might such a person do to try to live up to it?

5. Almost everyone has some kind of reputation, although a person's reputation at home, school, in the neighborhood, in clubs and on teams, or with friends may be quite different. What different kinds of *reputations* do some of your friends have? How does one get a reputation?

About Revenge

6. What incidents can you recall which aroused feelings of revenge in you?

7. One of comedian Jackie Gleason's often-used laugh lines is *"How sweet it is!"* What do you think the *"it"* refers to?

8. Most parents, religious leaders, and teachers use the saying *"Revenge is Mine," sayeth the Lord* to try to calm us down when we are bitter and feel like getting even. Why do you think this is or is not good advice? Why do you suppose it is so hard to follow such advice?

About Con Jobs

9. Have you been the victim of any con jobs? If so, what were they?

10. Not all con jobs are dishonest or criminal in the true legal sense. Instead, many con artists take advantage of a person's ignorance or naïveté and, with sly tricks, use information which only they have to their advantage. What's the worst thing about being conned like this when you realize there's nothing you can do about it?

III. PREREADING ACTIVITIES

The Prereading Activities which follow purpose to elicit *analogous* or *parallel* experiences from the reader's background so that he/she can identify more intensely with the *feelings* of the characters in the book—as they interact with other characters, situations, and events—as he/she reads and finds them familiar because they are but one step removed from the real occurrences in his/her life.

Name_____

Date_____

1. Historical Have-Nots

DIRECTIONS: As you know, there was no television in people's homes in the year 1900. What other things do you know about that most people in America DID NOT HAVE before 1900? Put an N on the line in front of each thing below WHICH YOU THINK MOST PEOPLE DIDN'T HAVE before 1900. Put a Y in front of those you think most people DID HAVE, and put an S on the lines in front of those you think are just plain SILLY!

__flashlights	__movies	__silver dollars
__telephones	__licorice	__radios
__gingersnaps	__department	__Monopoly
__post offices	stores	__gunnysacks
__baseball	__wrestling	__jawbreakers
__indoor toilets	__shots for	__telephones
__IQ tests	measles	__one-room
__electricity	__spankings in	schools
__curfews	school	__rock 'n' roll
__malnutrition	__Mickey Mouse	__automobiles
__ice cream	__newspapers	__bathing suits
		__Sears, Roebuck

(After reading the book, what changes would you make?)

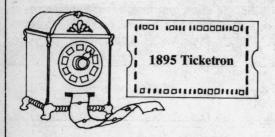

Name_____

Date_____

2.

1895 Ticketron

DIRECTIONS: Suddenly you find yourself back in the year 1895! It's Saturday morning and you've just earned five cents chopping and carrying in wood for your five regular customers, and you now want to have some fun spending it. As you walk down Main Street toward home, you notice a strange new invention on the sidewalk in front of GUS SWAKHAMMER'S GENERAL STORE. *It's a TICKETRON MACHINE which allows you to select a ticket for each penny you put in. All you do is turn the selector knob so that it points to the ticket you want, put in a penny, and take out your ticket. You decide to blow your whole bundle—all five pennies!* WHAT WILL YOUR CHOICES BE? *Remember, it's the year 1895, and as silly as some of the choices may seem to you now, you may have been very willing to spend twice that much back then. (1) Cut out the five tickets of your choice from those presented below. (2) Seal them up in an envelope until you have finished reading the book. (3) Then, open it up and see whether or not you have made good 1895 choices.*

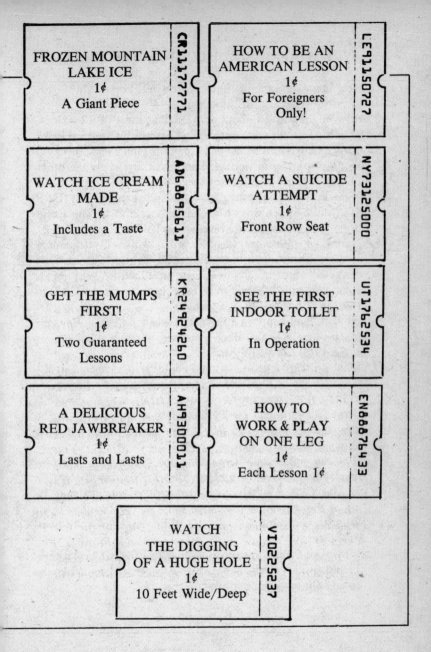

FROZEN MOUNTAIN LAKE ICE
1¢
A Giant Piece

CR)))???7)

HOW TO BE AN AMERICAN LESSON
1¢
For Foreigners Only!

LE9))50727

WATCH ICE CREAM MADE
1¢
Includes a Taste

AD6889S6))

WATCH A SUICIDE ATTEMPT
1¢
Front Row Seat

NY73)25000

GET THE MUMPS FIRST!
1¢
Two Guaranteed Lessons

KR24924260

SEE THE FIRST INDOOR TOILET
1¢
In Operation

UT)76253Ч

A DELICIOUS RED JAWBREAKER
1¢
Lasts and Lasts

AH93000))

HOW TO WORK & PLAY ON ONE LEG
1¢
Each Lesson 1¢

EN8887Ч433

WATCH THE DIGGING OF A HUGE HOLE
1¢
10 Feet Wide/Deep

VI0225237

IV. POSTREADING DISCUSSION QUESTIONS

1. How can you explain the way you felt about The Great Brain's revenge on Mr. Standish?
2. How might you go about proving that most of The Great Brain's successes were nothing but extraordinary good luck?
3. Basil Kokovinis took a lot of painful punishment because he followed the advice of The Great Brain. What other advice would *you* have suggested to Basil?
4. What reasons can you give that might explain why Basil Kokovinis' father was so proud and grateful to The Great Brain for getting his son beat up by bullies?
5. *The silent treatment* was the worst kind of punishment used by everyone in the Fitzgerald home. Why do you think the silent treatment can be so effective? Why do or don't you think that it may have been worse in Utah in 1896 than where you live today?
6. What do you suppose J.D. meant when he said, *"Revenge can be sour"*? What other instances of revenge going sour in the story can you describe?
7. What do you suppose Mamma could have meant when she said that Mr. Harvey didn't like kids because he had never had to put up with any of his own?
8. How do you think the Fitzgerald brothers arrived at the idea that *tolerance* is taught by fighting and whipping others?
9. How can you explain why such a nosey, caring, loving community as Adenville could have let such a tragedy happen to Abie Glassman? How can you explain your understanding of the way Abie Glassman felt?
10. Why do you think J.D. was so willing to help Andy commit suicide?
11. Why would you agree or disagree with J.D. that his brother, Tom D., The Great Brain, *was* a cheat and a crook and behaved in un-Christian ways?

V. HELPING CHILDREN TO REVEAL
THEIR COMPREHENSION

Characteristic T-Shirts

Name_____

Date_____

DIRECTIONS: Suppose Tom D. Fitzgerald's GREAT BRAIN had been the first to think of T-shirts with designs, slogans, and pictures appropriate to the beliefs, ideas, and accomplishments of their wearers on them? As you know, The Great Brain always seems to manage to get someone else to do most of the work for him and this time YOU ARE THAT PERSON! On the fronts of the T-shirts below, he wants you to PERSONALIZE one for different characters in the story, including The Great Brain himself, if you choose. Make sure your design, picture, and slogan are SPECIAL to the character you choose. In case you have trouble remembering, here are some of the names from the story you could choose from or add any others you like.

Sweyn, Tom, and John Fitzgerald—Sammy Leeds—Andy Anderson—Seth Smith—Pete Hanson—Basil Kokovinis—Mr. Standish—
Abie Glassman

_____'s
T-Shirt

_____'s
T-Shirt

_____'s
T-Shirt

_____'s
T-Shirt

_____'s
T-Shirt

2.

The Price Is Right!

DIRECTIONS: As you know, The Big Brain was a BIG wheeler and dealer until he reformed. In the story, he made a lot of bargains and deals with people who thought his PRICE RIGHT! Below are seven of Tom D.'s deals with a price tag attached to each one. Look at the list of "SHOPPERS" then study the items involved in his bargains. On each "Price Tag" write the name of the shopper or shoppers and then describe what you think the deal was between each one and The Great Brain.

LIST OF SHOPPERS

J. D. Fitzgerald
Andy Anderson
Mr. Standish
Mr. Kokovinis
Basil Kokovinis
Sammy Leeds
Seth Smith
Pete Hanson

Special Teaching
of the Handicapped

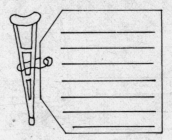

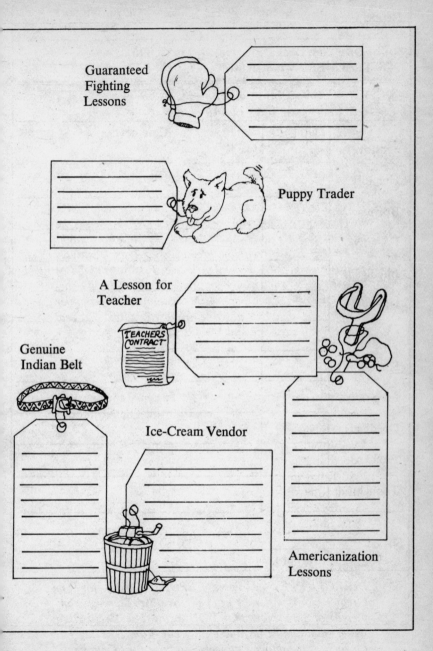

Guaranteed Fighting Lessons

Puppy Trader

A Lesson for Teacher

TEACHERS CONTRACT

Genuine Indian Belt

Ice-Cream Vendor

Americanization Lessons

139

3.

| Report Card | Adenville Public School | Calvin Whitlock, Pres. |
| | Adenville, Utah | School Board |

FOR: Tom Dennis Fitzgerald—1895–1896
TEACHER: Mr. Standish

A = 90-100   B = 80-89   C = 65-79
D = 55-64   E = 45-54   F = 0-44

	Grade	Comments
Sensitive		
Humility		
Brave		
Friendly		
Intelligent		
Happy		
Generous		
Honest		
Forgiving		
Obedient		
Proud		
Thoughtful		

Signed: _____   Date: _____
      (your name)

DIRECTIONS: The above REPORT CARD for The Great Brain is different from the one Mr. Standish completed for him. Now that YOU know The Great Brain better than almost anyone else, grade Tom D. Fitzgerald on each of the above "subjects" and use the "Comments" column to explain briefly how you arrived at his grade.

VI. RELATED-TO-READING EXPERIENCES

1. **Ice-Cream Maker**
   Learn to make ice cream the way The Great Brain and his brothers did for Sunday dinner! Invent your own flavors!

2. **A Spelunking Search**
   Find out what *spelunking* is and ask a *spelunker* to tell your class of some of the fun and dangers he/she has had.

3. **A Religious Quest**
   What can you learn about the Mormons and their church in addition to what J.D. has told you in this book? Why was such a large percent of Adenville's population Mormon? How do their beliefs differ from yours? Visit a Mormon church and talk with some of their church leaders to collect your data.

THE SECRET GARDEN

by

FRANCES HODGSON BURNETT

Illustrated by Tasha Tudor

I. THE STORY

"It was the sweetest, most mysterious-looking place anyone could imagine. The high walls which shut it in were covered with the leafless stems of climbing roses which were so thick that they were matted together. . . . No wonder it is still," Mary whispered. . . . *"I am the first person who has spoken in here for ten years."* When Mary Lennox moves into Misselthwaite Manor—a huge estate—to live with her uncle, everybody said she was the most disagreeable-looking child ever seen. It was true, too. *The Secret Garden* is the story of Mary, a cross, self-centered little girl, and Colin, a pampered, invalid boy who learn compassion and generosity with the help of a robin; Mar-centered little girl, and Colin, a pampered, invalid boy, who loves and is loved by all living things; and the quiet miracles of nature that they discover in an abandoned garden.

II. PREREADING DISCUSSION QUESTIONS

The questions which follow are illustrative of the kinds which teachers can prepare for the purpose of releasing children to reveal how they feel about some of the larger ideas and bigger meanings contained in the book before it is read by the children.

About Unwanted Children
　　1. How many different reasons can you think of that might explain why some children are convinced that their parents don't care about them?

2. What things can you think of that cause some people to treat children cruelly?

3. When children are disliked or even unwanted by their parents, what do you think are some of the cruelest things you've heard of which they've done to them?

4. Some children are spoiled by giving them servants to wait on them and allowing them to do or to have anything they want. In what ways do you think that this could be proof that such children really are *unwanted* in such families?

5. What do you think can happen rather suddenly in happy families that would make a child feel unloved and unwanted?

About Worrying

6. Some worriers become angry when someone tells them they are silly for worrying and that they should just enjoy themselves and face and solve problems when and *if* they occur! But the worriers argue that a person should always be thinking ahead, preparing for the unexpected so that it will be possible to *make a good decision quickly*. They claim that's the *only* real way a person can relax and enjoy himself! What opinions do you have about *the worrier* or *the nonworrier*?

7. Why do you think people often surprise themselves by *succeeding* in doing something which they were convinced they could not do?

8. What are some of your experiences that would prove that this old saying, *"Where there's a will, there's a way!"* is true?

9. Some people talk about having a bad reputation which is hard to *live down*. What examples can you give about how a person tries to live with or live down a *bad* reputation? Why might a person *want* to have a bad reputation?

10. How do you think it could be possible for a person to have a poor personality *and not know it*?

III. PREREADING ACTIVITIES

The Prereading Activities which follow purpose to elicit *analogous* or *parallel* experiences from the reader's background so that he/she can identify more intensely with the *feelings* of

Name _____

Date _____

1. **Match 'n' Mark**

DIRECTIONS: Read each of the statements below and decide which of the four choices best MATCHES HOW YOU THINK, or FEEL, or WOULD ACT. (There are NO right or wrong choices!) *Then, when you've decided the best match, take a red pen or pencil and mark it. After you've finished reading* The Secret Garden, *take a blue pen or pencil and REMARK each of the items so that the choices now MATCH THE PEOPLE and HAPPENINGS in the story.*

1. If you were asked to baby-sit with someone who was a spoiled brat, what would you do if he/she threw a temper tantrum for no reason at all?
(a) Give him/her your baby-sitting money to stop, (b) throw a tantrum of your own that's worse, (c) try to reason and talk him/her out of it, (d) threaten to call his/her parents and leave.
2. If you suddenly found yourself living with your aunt and uncle whom you've never met before, in a large mansion in which you've never been before, and, although you've heard

the characters in the book—as they interact with other characters, situations, and events—as he/she reads and finds them familiar because they are but one step removed from the real occurrences in his/her life.

footsteps, voices, and crying upstairs, you are told it's your imagination and that no one is up there, what would you do? (a) investigate in the middle of the night, (b) believe what you are told, (c) call the police, (d) mind your own business.

3. Suppose you had to spend many weeks by yourself with no one to talk to or play with. Which of the following would you choose to help pass the time?
(a) Books to read, (b) a guitar, (c) a horse and saddle, (d) lots of seeds and land for a garden.

4. While visiting your grandparents you discover a room in the house that's been locked tight for thirteen years, the key hidden, and everyone forbidden to enter. Then, while watching a squirrel bury a nut, you notice him uncover an old rusty key. You clean it off and try it in the lock of the "mystery door"—and it works! What do you do then?
(a) Give the key to your grandparents, (b) bury it again, (c) open the door and go in, (d) ask for permission to explore it.

5. You have just discovered something very important—too important to keep to yourself, yet a secret that can't be told for six months. Which one of the following people would you trust with such a secret?
(a) A strange young person your age who loves and is loved by all animals and living things, (b) an old, grouchy handyman who never speaks to anyone, (c) a young person your age who has been sick in bed since birth and hates all grownups, (d) a poor, young, and not very bright cleaning woman.

2.

How to Spoil a Child in Six Easy Steps

DIRECTIONS: Think of someone your age who is polite, well-liked, cooperative, popular, and unselfish. The problem is, this person is JUST TOO PERFECT! Just too good, and as a result, he/she is miserable. Dr. Hedda Shrink, world famous psychiatrist, has decided that the only cure for your friend would be to SPOIL him/her a little, but it needs to be done quickly. You have been selected for the job and must come up with SIX EASY WAYS TO SPOIL YOUR FRIEND. Think about this almost-perfect person. (It should be someone you know well enough—it could even be you, if you want.) What would be your plan of action?

1. _____

_____

2. _____

_____

3. _____

_____

4. _____

_____

5. _____

_____

6. _____

_____

3. **It Must Be Magic (or is it?)**

DIRECTIONS: Whenever something happens that seems mysterious or unbelievable or unexplainable, many people quickly say "IT'S MAGIC!" Put an M on the line in front of each of the items below which you feel COULD BE MAGIC.

_____1. A person who can communicate with birds and wild animals.

_____2. A hateful, selfish person becomes kind and loving.

_____3. A person who becomes well and healthy after doctors tried everything and predicted an early death.

_____4. A bird that shows you the key to a secret treasure.

_____5. A person who ALWAYS thinks of many different ways to do nice, kind things for others.

_____6. When valuable, beautiful things are made out of nothing.

_____7. When winter disappears and spring flowers bloom.

_____8. The healing power of fresh air and sunshine.

IV. POSTREADING DISCUSSION QUESTIONS

1. When Mary met her uncle, Mr. Craven, for the first time and asked him for "a bit of earth," why were or weren't you surprised to find him acting the way he did toward Mary?

2. Colin and Mary were both spoiled children, but they each were spoiled differently and for different reasons. How might you explain why neither of them *knew they were spoiled?*

3. If someone told you that the only "disease" that caused Colin's illness was *gossip and rumor,* why would you agree or disagree?

147

4. How many examples can you give that would show that Mary Lennox and Colin Craven *came alive with the Secret Garden?*

5. Everyone, even strict Mrs. Medlock, grouchy Ben Weatherstaff, and suspicious Dr. Craven, loved and trusted Dickon. How many reasons can you give that would explain why people felt this way about Dickon?

6. How can you explain why everyone seemed to be so afraid of Mr. Craven?

7. How do you suppose the old saying, *"Where there's a will, there's a way!"* might have been written especially for young Colin Craven?

8. Why do you think some people would say that *boredom* and *curiosity* more than anything else caused "Mistress Mary Quite Contrary" to change so quickly for the better?

9. On page 238, Colin tells Mary, Dickon, and Ben that a boy is an animal. What do you think he meant by that?

10. Why do you think it was so difficult for Colin to pretend he was sick, after he was well?

V. HELPING CHILDREN TO REVEAL THEIR COMPREHENSION

1.

PERSONAL—KEYS

Name_____

Date_____

DIRECTIONS: The name of one of the characters you read about in The Secret Garden *appears on each of the "KEYS" below. On each of the KEY TAGS attached to these keys, there is space for you to write those PERSONALITY TRAITS which you feel best identifies each of these characters. Select your traits for each character from the "WORD KEYS" list. Even though you will find MORE words than you need, you are permitted to use a word ONLY ONCE. However, you may substitute YOUR OWN WORDS, if you choose to do so.*

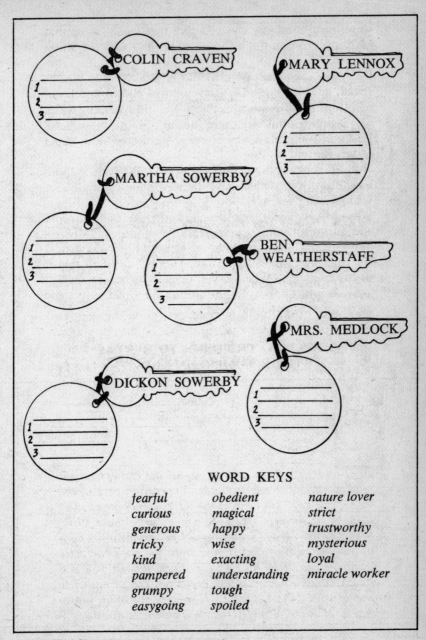

COLIN CRAVEN

1 _____
2 _____
3 _____

MARY LENNOX

1 _____
2 _____
3 _____

MARTHA SOWERBY

1 _____
2 _____
3 _____

BEN WEATHERSTAFF

1 _____
2 _____
3 _____

MRS. MEDLOCK

1 _____
2 _____
3 _____

DICKON SOWERBY

1 _____
2 _____
3 _____

WORD KEYS

fearful   *obedient*   *nature lover*
curious   *magical*   *strict*
generous   *happy*   *trustworthy*
tricky   *wise*   *mysterious*
kind   *exacting*   *loyal*
pampered   *understanding* *miracle worker*
grumpy   *tough*
easygoing   *spoiled*

Name_____

Date_____

2.

DIRECTIONS: Now that you've finished reading The Secret Garden, suppose that at the very beginning of the story—before any of the action begins—DICKON Sowerby, MARY Lennox, COLIN Craven, and ARCHIBALD Craven (Colin's father) come to you to have their FORTUNES told! Remembering what kind of people they were at the beginning and, also, what happens to them, you accept the challenge. One by one they each come to you, you look into your crystal ball, and you tell their fortunes—AND EACH ONE COMES TRUE!

DICKON SOWERBY _____

_____

_____

_____

_____

_____

_____

_____

MARY
LENNOX

_____

_____

_____

_____

_____

_____

ARCHIBALD
CRAVEN

_____

_____

_____

_____

_____

_____

COLIN
CRAVEN

_____

_____

_____

_____

_____

_____

_____

3.

I've Got a Secret . . .

DIRECTIONS: As you know, now that you've finished reading The Secret Garden, *many of the people in the story had SECRETS just as the garden did. Suppose you picked up the pillow in which the mice family had once lived and found a ring of KEYS . . . each one of them to a DOOR belonging to one of the characters in the story and behind which is hidden that character's SECRET. You have opened each of the DOORS below, and on the mysterious lines you find there, you are to write what you think that person's SECRET is and why you think it was or was not necessary to have.*

DICKON'S

SECRET

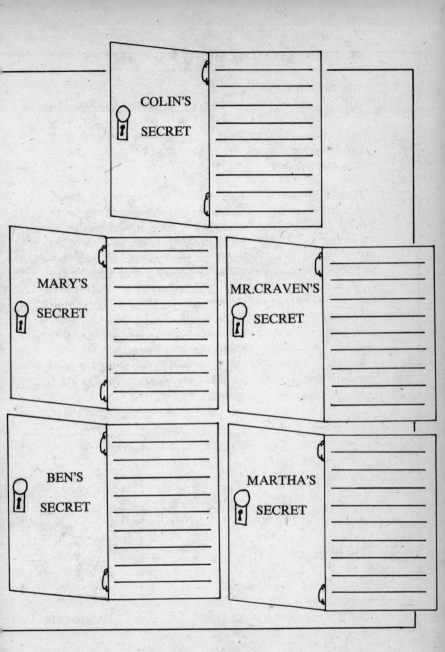

COLIN'S SECRET

MARY'S SECRET

MR.CRAVEN'S SECRET

BEN'S SECRET

MARTHA'S SECRET

VI. RELATED-TO-READING EXPERIENCES

1. **Garden Magic**

   All you need to enter your very own "Secret Garden" is a pair of MAGIC SCISSORS, construction paper (use various colors, if possible, for a colorful garden), and, like Mary Lennox and Colin Craven, a belief in your own magic powers!

   DIRECTIONS:
   1. *Fold a piece of construction paper.*
   2. *Select one of the magic things below you wish to have in your garden.*
   3. *Study the simple lines on each of the magic patterns below. (If your belief in your magic powers is strong enough you will find it UNNECESSARY to draw these lines on your paper first!)*
   4. *Hold the folded paper with the fold horizontal and toward you.*
   5. *Let your magic eye guide the scissors as they create your SECRET GARDEN.*

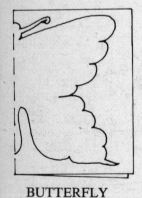
BUTTERFLY

TULIP

LOVEBIRDS

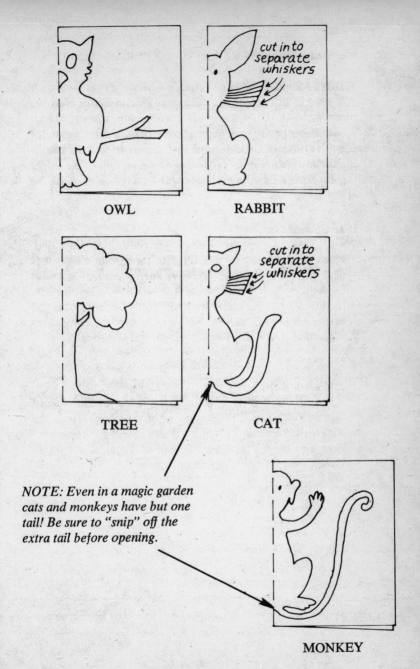

OWL

RABBIT
cut into separate whiskers

TREE

CAT
cut into separate whiskers

NOTE: *Even in a magic garden cats and monkeys have but one tail! Be sure to "snip" off the extra tail before opening.*

MONKEY

155

2. Growin' Magic

DIRECTIONS: Watch Nature's power right in your own house! You will need (a) a sponge (it can be an old one, but be sure you rinse it well with fresh water), (b) an old saucer or foil dish large enough to hold the sponge, (c) an old dish or shallow foil dish about 6 to 8 inches in diameter, (d) two clean glasses or clean, empty glass jars (pint size), and (e) a piece of cotton.

1. Sponge Garden

Soak the sponge with water until it is saturated. Place it in the saucer and fill with more water until it is near the brim or edge. (Always keep plenty of water in the saucer; it isn't necessary to dampen the sponge any further.) Sprinkle some birdseed (or grass seed) on top of the sponge. Place the "Sponge Garden" on a windowsill where it will get some daylight and watch it grow!

2. Carrot Tops

Fill the 6-8 inch dish about three-fourths full of water. Place the tops of two or three carrots into the water. Put the dish in a place where it will get some sunlight and keep it at least half-full of water at all times. Watch the green tops sprout and grow!

3. Sweet Potato Fun

Place one end of a sweet potato into an empty tumbler or clean glass jar. Fill it with fresh water until about two-thirds of the sweet potato is underwater. Put it in a sunny place and watch it grow and grow. Once it begins to grow, you may keep the jar or tumbler nearly full of water.

4. Mysterious Lima

Fill an empty tumbler or clean 8-ounce jar about two-thirds full of fresh water. On top of the water, gently spread a generous piece of cotton. On top of the cotton, carefully place three or four dry lima beans. Put the jar or tumbler on a window ledge where it will receive some daylight. Watch your own magic beanstalk grow and grow.

THE HOUSE OF WINGS

by BETSY BYARS

Illustrated by Daniel Schwartz

I. THE STORY

The sight of his grandfather made Sammy sick. Furious with his parents for leaving him behind, hating the old man, Sammy ran. He could hear his grandfather behind him, hear his cries of *"Wait, boy."* Then, quietly, in the midst of the chase, a wounded crane appeared, alone in the woods, pathetic, beautiful. The old man called softly for the boy to come back, and somehow Sammy knew his grandfather was calling him for something more important than their feud.

A few days can be a long time—long enough to tame a crane, long enough for a boy to learn to love.

II. PREREADING DISCUSSION QUESTIONS

The questions which follow are illustrative of the kinds which teachers can prepare for the purpose of releasing children to reveal how they feel *about some of the larger ideas and bigger meanings contained in the book* before it is read by the children.

About Parental Decisions

1. What reasons can you give that might explain why some parents would find it necessary to send their children away to live with someone else for a long period of time *without asking or explaining the reasons* to them?

2. What things have caused shouting matches between you and your parents?
3. What can you reveal which you feel bugs most young people as far as parents are concerned?
4. How would you argue that parents have or haven't the right to know where you are going and with whom when you leave the house?

About Older Generations

5. Why do you think young people seem to like grandparents so much?
6. Why do you think young people often get along so well with their grandparents rather than with their parents?
7. Why do you think grandparents have or do not have more patience than parents?

About Apprehensions and Bluffs

8. Some people are discouraged very easily and quit, while others will never seem to give up. Why do you think people differ like this? Why do you think most people give up more quickly in *unknown* situations and with *new* things than with something they are familiar?
9. What do you think causes some people to bluff or fake it? What causes others to stretch the truth or tell tall tales to help themselves out?
10. Some young people fake it or bluff it when they want to make an impression, or don't want to show that they DON'T know something which they *should* know, and/or to keep from feeling ashamed. When do you think bluffing is justified? When do you think bluffing is a dishonest cop-out? How many examples can you give?

III. PREREADING ACTIVITIES

The Prereading Activities which follow purpose to elicit *analogous* or *parallel* experiences from the reader's background so that he/she can identify more intensely with the *feelings* of the

---

Name_____

Date_____

1. **Hidden Feelings**

DIRECTIONS: When some people are afraid, unhappy, or terribly embarrassed, they frequently try to hide their REAL feelings from anyone and everyone. In each of the following situations described below, tell how you (or a friend) might HIDE YOUR FEELINGS.

SITUATION ONE: A group of older and bigger tough kids is standing in front of the supermarket making rude comments about people as they pass. You have to go into that supermarket to buy a few things for your mother.

_____

_____

_____

SITUATION TWO: You have just overheard your two best friends say that they wouldn't be caught dead wearing the clothes your parents send you to school in. Then a few minutes later you join them.

_____

_____

_____

characters in the book—as they interact with other characters, situations, and events—as he/she reads and finds them familiar because they are but one step removed from the real occurrences in his/her life.

SITUATION THREE: Your brother, who is a year younger than you and who has been crippled since birth, has just broken the ashtray which took you weeks to make for your father. You had intended to give it to him for his birthday.

_____

_____

_____

SITUATION FOUR: You are trying to impress your teacher and classmates by telling a long story made up completely of lies. You have everyone fooled until you tell about the many times TV comedian Paul Lynde came to your house for dinner in Cleveland, Ohio—his home town—before he became famous. Then your teacher points out that she went to school with Paul Lynde in his hometown of Mount Vernon, Ohio.

_____

_____

_____

SITUATION FIVE: You have invited your three best friends for a treat at the QUIK-BURGER Drive-Inn. After all of you have ordered, you discover that you are seventy-five cents short.

_____

_____

_____

Name_____

Date_____

2. **Mind-Blowing Reminders**

> *DIRECTIONS: Almost all young people are upset by GENTLE REMINDERS which parents, grandparents, and older sisters and brothers constantly give. Some of these reminders are more frequent than others; some are more irritating. Read the list of reminders below. After each, put an X in the appropriate column to indicate how much of a MIND-BLOWER each REMINDER is to YOU.*

	ALWAYS	SOMETIMES	NEVER
1. "You should save your money for things you'll really want someday instead of throwing it away on all those rock records and tapes."			
2. "You promised us if we'd let you have a pet, you'd take care of it."			
3. "Don't you think you should do your homework before you start watching TV?"			

	ALWAYS	SOMETIMES	NEVER
4. "It's way past your bedtime . . ."			
5. "When's the last time you brushed your teeth?"			
6. "Have you cleaned up your room yet . . . ?"			
7. "You're old enough to know that all that junk you eat isn't good for you . . ."			
8. "You're certainly big enough to know that you can't always have things go the way you want them to . . ."			
9. "Don't you think it's about time you apologize . . .?"			
10. "There's only one thing we expect of you and that is that you always tell us the truth."			
11. "Comb your hair out of your eyes or else get a haircut!"			
12. "Do you know what time it is?"			

IV. POSTREADING DISCUSSION QUESTIONS

1. What reasons can you think of that might explain why Sammy kept calling his grandfather a liar *even after he knew the old man was telling the truth?*

2. Why do you suppose Sammy's grandfather didn't poke fun at him or try to put him down for lying or bluffing his way through things he knew nothing about?

3. Near the end of the story (p. 141), while Sammy is looking at his grandfather in a funny way, he wonders *"how it is possible to hate a person in the middle of one morning, and then to find in the middle of the next morning that you love this same person."* What do you think you might say to Sammy, if you had the chance to try to explain why this happened to him?

4. Some readers of this book might argue that *it was something else,* and not the unusual discovery of the sandhill crane, that stopped Sammy from running away from his grandfather. Suppose you agree. What could this "something else" have been?

5. The crane which Sammy and his grandfather found was blind, it wouldn't eat, didn't seem to care about anything, and wouldn't do anything to help itself. How do you think that Sammy and the crane were alike?

6. On page 74, Sammy's grandfather told him: *"Every one of them birds that stayed with me is more real to me than the people I've known."* Why do you think the old man felt like this? Later on in the story, why do you think that Sammy wanted his grandfather to know him the way he knew his birds?

7. How many reasons can you give that would explain why Sammy kept lying to his grandfather throughout the whole story even though he quickly learned that his bluffs didn't seem to influence the old man one way or the other?

8. The only time Sammy's grandfather lost his temper was the time Sammy (p. 48) said he hoped the crane would die. Then, later on that same day (p. 94) when the old man was talking about killing the crane to "put it out of its misery," Sammy began to plead for its life! Knowing these two characters as well as you do now, how is it possible to understand why they seemed to change so radically and so quickly?

9. Why do you think the complete *freedom* Sammy's grandfather gave him was or was not the best way to treat Sammy?

V. HELPING CHILDREN TO REVEAL
THEIR COMPREHENSION

Name_____

Date_____

1. | **The Lie Detector**

DIRECTIONS: *Throughout the story, Sammy tried to BLUFF his way through situations which he knew nothing about—perhaps to save face or to fool his grandfather or, perhaps, to hide his fear or anger. In other situations, he lied; and in others, he told the truth. Listed below are statements about Sammy—what he said, thought, or did. In the appropriate box following each, put an X to show whether YOU THINK Sammy was just BLUFFING, telling the TRUTH, or LYING. After you finish, you might like to go back to the pages in the story to see if you DETECTED Sammy's lies as accurately as you could.*

	A BLUFF	A LIE	THE TRUTH
1. Sammy wanted his grandfather to know him the way he knew his birds. (P. 140.)			
2. "I can't swim very well now, but I'll get better." (P. 142.)			
3. "I never heard of any crane getting to be twenty-one . . . Fourteen maybe, or fifteen . . ." (P. 42.)			
4. "No, I never had a rooster, but I *could* have had one if I'd wanted it but—" (P. 42.)			

	A BLUFF	A LIE	THE TRUTH
5. "I don't care if the crane does die, he's nothing but a bird." (P. 45.)			
6. "It would serve you right if I did run away to Detroit . . ." (P. 50.)			
7. (Sammy's grandfather said: "I'll get the crane—one way or another.") And Sammy said to himself, "That's what I'm afraid of." (P. 57.)			
8. (Sammy's grandfather said: "I reckon you're hungry, boy, aren't you, not having any breakfast?") "Well, I'm not *that* hungry," Sammy said. (P. 97.)			
9. When Sammy's grandfather told him to take the bandanna from his hip pocket and blindfold the crane, Sammy said, "Well, where is the bandanna? I don't see any bandanna." (P. 68.)			
10. The owl swooped over to the table. ("He ain't going to hurt you," his grandfather said.) "I know that," Sammy answered. (P. 100.)			

2. **A Postcard from Detroit**

DIRECTIONS: The day after the story ends, Sammy gets a postcard from his parents who reached Detroit. What do you think they need and want to say to him? How do you think they will say it? Put yourself in the place of Sammy's mother or father and write him a postcard. Why not give Sammy a last name and a real address, too?

```
┌─────────────────────────────────────────────────────────┐
│                                    PostCard      ┌──────┐ │
│                                                  │Place │ │
│                                                  │Stamp │ │
│                                                  │Here  │ │
│                                                  └──────┘ │
│                                    _____    │
│                                                           │
│                                    _____    │
│                                                           │
│                                    _____    │
│                                                           │
│                                          _____       │
│                                                           │
│                                                           │
└─────────────────────────────────────────────────────────┘
```

3. **A Telegram from Sammy**

DIRECTIONS: Telegrams are short, fast messages which are sent in emergencies or in instances to let someone know something very quickly. People who send telegrams try to use as few words as possible since they are charged for each word used. With the help of his grandfather, Sammy found out his parents' Detroit address; and since they didn't yet have a telephone, he knew the news he had for them was important enough to put into a telegram. What do you think Sammy would say to them? How would he say it in fifty words or less? Print the message on the telegram below.

168

| TIME: | **WESTERN UNION** ~Telegram~ | DATE: |

FROM:

4. **Three-way Conversation at Midnight!**

Sammy was tired when they arrived at the strange
Ohio farm of his grandfather; so he went to bed. As you
know, during the night, his parents made an important
decision that would change Sammy's life in such a way
that he would never be the same again! The author
doesn't let us know this conversation but anyone reading
this book will surely have several ideas about what was
discussed between Sammy's parents and his grandfather. What questions would have been raised and by
whom? What would some of the answers have been?
Who would have made these suggestions? An exciting
way to record this three-way conversation would be to
write it in play-script form:

FATHER. _____

GRANDFATHER. _____

MOTHER. _____

(and so on)

VI. RELATED-TO-READING EXPERIENCES

1. **A House of Synonyms**

   In the story you've just read, Sammy's grandfather's house was, indeed, a HOUSE OF WINGS, as it became a part-time home for many kinds of birds: geese, owls, parrots, canaries, cranes, blackbirds, wild ducks, redbirds, thrashers, and so forth. *When groups of animals are together, there are SPECIAL TERMS we use to describe them such as "drey" of squirrels, a "gang" of elk, a "pride" of lions, and a "gam" of whales. When FLOCKS of birds or other winged creatures (such as insects) are together, there also are SPECIAL WORDS or synonyms for "flock" which we use to describe them. Some of these synonyms are common and well-known; others are pretty old—rarely used anymore—and can be found only in a very large dictionary. Even so, if you know something about the bird, it is interesting how appropriate their group names really are. How well can you match the "WINGS" below with their SYNONYMS?*

_____of geese	A SWARM
_____of larks	A NYE
_____of peacocks	A FLIGHT
_____of starlings	A HOST
_____of ravens	A PITYING
_____of crows	A WATCH
_____of bees	A BEVY
_____of pheasants	A GAGGLE
_____of doves	A MURDER
_____of locusts	A MURMURATION
_____of eagles	AN AERIE
_____of quail	AN UNKINDNESS
_____of nightingales	A MUSTER
_____of swallows	A COVEY

2. It's for the Birds

In the "birdhouse" below, there are sixteen birds! Their names can be found in the "maze" of letters below, but you'll have to bird-watch more cleverly than you've ever done before since some of the names will read backward, some forward, others up, down, or on the diagonal. Some may cross or overlap other letters—but in no instance, more than a single letter. You will find it helpful to keep track by drawing a line around each bird as you find it.

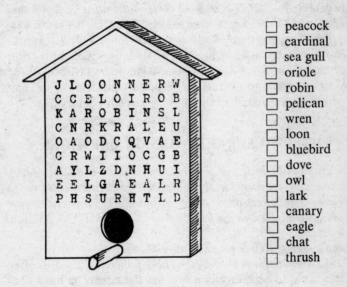

J L O O N N E R W
C C E L O I R O B
K A R O B I N S L
C N R K R A L E U
O A O D C Q V A E
C R W I I O C G B
A Y L Z D N H U I
E E L G A E A L R
P H S U R H T L D

☐ peacock
☐ cardinal
☐ sea gull
☐ oriole
☐ robin
☐ pelican
☐ wren
☐ loon
☐ bluebird
☐ dove
☐ owl
☐ lark
☐ canary
☐ eagle
☐ chat
☐ thrush

J.T.

by JANE WAGNER

Pictures by Gordon Parks, Jr.

I. THE STORY

To the guys on the block, J.T. is the kid who stole the radio out of the red convertible before they could get to it. His neighbor, Mrs. Morris, declares him a first-class nuisance. His mother is bewildered— *"He's just gone bad, that's all. . . . Lyin' and stealin' and I don't know what all else."* But all the sensitivity, responsibility, and care of which the ten-year-old J. T. Gamble is capable emerges when he finds an old, one-eyed, badly hurt alley cat. J.T. takes on a new dimension as he lavishes all the love he is unable to express to people around him on the battered cat he has found in the junk-filled empty lot.

II. PREREADING DISCUSSION QUESTIONS

The questions which follow are illustrative of the kinds which teachers can prepare for the purpose of releasing children to reveal how they feel *about some of the larger ideas and bigger meanings contained in the book* before it is read by the children.

About Parents, Relatives, and Other Things

1. The common expression *"Like father, like son!"* is often used to explain why a boy has the talents he has or behaves in the way he does. As you think about the father-son combinations you know, what do you think about the accuracy of this statement? How true do you think it is?
2. Why do you think so many young people often get along better with their grandparents than their parents?
3. There are many different circumstances which cause some children to be raised by only one parent. How

172

many different reasons can you think of? Some people feel that a child being raised for most of his/her life by just one parent has a serious disadvantage—that his/her chances for a successful, happy future are very slim. Why would you agree or disagree with this idea?

4. Suppose that for the next year or two circumstances would occur whereby you would have only one of your parents responsible for raising you. What do you think would be several of your parent's most worrisome problems? What do you think would be your most difficult problems?

About Pets

5. What reasons can you think of that would explain why many parents *do not* want their children to have pets?

6. Why do so many young people want to have a pet more than anything in the world?

7. Some people seem to think that, while it's good for people to have pets, *it's not a good idea to love them too much!* What do you suppose this means? What is "too much"? Why would you agree or disagree with this belief?

About Stealing

8. Even though our society considers it wrong, some people steal because they are so desperate or because their needs are beyond hope! Yet, other people have other reasons for stealing. How many different reasons can you give?

9. Why do you think it is (1) worse, (2) not as bad, or (3) no different to steal from one's relatives than from a stranger?

III. PREREADING ACTIVITIES

The Prereading Activities which follow purpose to elicit *analogous* or *parallel* experiences from the reader's background so that he/she can identify more intensely with the *feelings* of the

characters in the book—as they interact with other characters, situations, and events—as he/she reads and finds them familiar because they are but one step removed from the real occurrences in his/her life.

1.   **Here Comes the Judge!**

LET YOUR CONSCIENCE BE THE JUDGE!

DIRECTIONS: Different people would "judge" the rightness or wrongness of each of the below situations in different ways because not all of us have the same ideas, backgrounds, values, or beliefs. Probably, in the strict legal and/or moral sense, most people would agree that all of these examples are "wrong," but WHICH WOULD BOTHER YOUR CONSCIENCE THE MOST? THE LEAST? By putting the numerals 1, 2, 3, and so forth in the blanks in front of each situation, re-arrange these statements to show which would bother YOUR conscience the most (#1) to those which would bother your conscience the least.

_____   Ripping off a fat cat's bread as he sits in front of you in a movie theater.

_____   Charging something to your parents' account at the drugstore without telling them.

_____   Borrowing some money from your mother's purse without asking.

_____   Keeping a cute puppy that follows you home even though it has an identification tag on its collar.

_____   Stealing a baseball mitt from a sports store.

_____   Taking a classmate's transistor radio she's left in her desk.

_____   Cutting school and lying to your teacher about it.

_____   Taking a purse left on a department store counter just minutes before someone you know is a thief steals it.

_____   Lying to your mother when she asks where you've been and why you are late.

---

2. Bully-ometer

DIRECTIONS: Make a bar graph which shows how YOU FEEL, on a scale of 1 to 10, about the kinds of things BULLIES do to people your age.

1 = just a harmless, silly prank
10 = cruel and evil, unfit for society

BULLIES' ANTICS	0	1	2	3	4	5	6	7	8	9	10
1. Spraying cola in your face.											
2. Throwing stones at your pet cat.											
3. Threats to beat you up, or to get you.											
4. Mimicking you and making fun of you.											
5. Frightening your little sister.											
6. Poisoning your dog to get even with you.											
7. Calling you and your relatives dirty names.											
8. Lying to get you into trouble in school.											

0　1　2　3　4　5　6　7　8　9　10

IV. POSTREADING DISCUSSION QUESTIONS

1. Why do Mr. and Mrs. Rosen seem to have a change of heart toward J. T. Gamble?

2. How many reasons can you think of that would explain why J.T. left the radio with Bones in the oven of the old abandoned stove?

3. Why do you suppose J.T. pouted and seemed almost angry with the kitten Mr. Rosen brought him as a Christmas present even though his mother and Mama Melcy approved?

4. Whether it's a book or movie, an animal or person, or a thing or place, it is doubtful that anyone or anything is 100 percent bad or 100 percent good. Yet, when Rodeen Gamble, J.T.'s mother, says: *"He's just gone bad, that's all. . . . Lyin' and stealin' and I don't know what all else."* it seems as if she's convinced he's 99 percent (if not 100 percent) hopelessly BAD! Now that you know J.T. so well, what are some of the *good* and *positive* things you could say to Mrs. Gamble to help her restore her faith in him?

V. HELPING CHILDREN TO REVEAL
THEIR COMPREHENSION

1. **Reformer-of-the-Month Award**

Rodeen Gamble, Mama Melcy, and Abe and Sarah Rosen have decided that J.T.'s change deserves some recognition, praise, and encouragement, so they had three "Merit Medals" made especially for him. At a special meat-loaf banquet, prepared by Mama Melcy and at which Mrs. Arnold and Mr. and Mrs. Rosen were honored guests, J.T. was awarded these three medals for three "unusually fine traits." What trait do you think was printed on each of the medals? (Remember who's presenting them to J.T.!) What picture or design is on each? How are they colored?

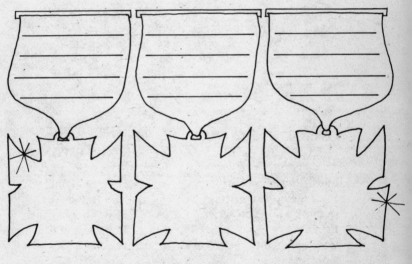

Presented to J.T. by
Abe and Sarah Rosen

Presented to J.T. by
Mama Melcy

Presented to J.T. by
Rodeen Gamble

2. **Countdown for Bones!**

... AND THEN THERE WERE NONE!
(Bones's Nine-Life Countdown)

DIRECTIONS: As you remember, when J.T. found BONES, he was in pretty bad shape! Undoubtedly he had lost some of his nine lives up to that moment although the author doesn't tell us anything about that. The rest is sadly clear, however, as one by one Bones's nine lives dwindle down to . . . none when he is hit by the car. Below you will find two lists. One is called:
"POSSIBLE CAUSE FOR ONE CAT LIFE"
The other is called:
"PERSON, ANIMAL, OR THING RESPONSIBLE"
Bones lost the first three of his nine lives before the story begins, so they are completed for you. Complete Bones's life and death countdown by connecting the appropriate CAUSE with the person, animal, or thing which you think is RESPONSIBLE.

POSSIBLE CAUSE FOR ONE CAT LIFE	PERSON, ANIMAL, OR THING RESPONSIBLE
—transistor radio	—Rodeen Gamble
—cold, snowy weather	—The Rosens
—wounds and scratches from fighting	—December weather
—loss of credit at grocery store	—Boomer and Claymore
—detained after school	—another tomcat
—told about J.T. getting tuna	—Mrs. Arnold

BONES

9	hit by falling stones	collapsing house wall	9
8	broken leg	hit by bicycle	8
7	hit hard with broom	Mrs. Morris	7
6			6
5			5
4			4
3			3
2			2
1			1
0	struck by car	hit-and-run driver	0

3. J.T.'s Christmas Composition

For many reasons J.T. thought Mrs. Arnold's assignment stupid and something he just could not do. But now, he seems to be a new person. Suppose Mrs. Arnold gave him a second chance to write the composition he couldn't do before (p. 90), now that things look brighter and better. Write the kind of composition for Mrs. Arnold which you think J.T. might have written.

Dec. 21, 197___

WHAT CHRISTMAS MEANS TO ME

by J. T. Gamble

VI. RELATED-TO-READING EXPERIENCES

1.   Pet-owner Survey

Ask as many of the pet owners in your school as you can how they got their pets. How many of them adopted strays? How many were purchased? How many were gifts? How many were obtained from an animal shelter? How many had difficulty convincing their parents to allow them to have a pet? What names do these pets have? What troubles have the pets caused their owners? What pleasures?

2.   Jeffie Michael Strikes Again!

Jeffie Michael (p. 70) admitted to J.T. that he was the one who drew one of the Wise Men on a *motorcycle!* Suppose Jeffie decides to change the "mode of transportation" of the other two Wise Men! Take another look at the picture on page 36, then pretending you are Jeffie Michael, get your crayons and draw the other two.

THE NIGHT DADDY

by MARIA GRIPE

Illustrated by Harald Gripe

I. THE STORY

Julia's mother, a nurse on the night shift, wants a companion for her young daughter. She advertises in the newspaper:

> EASY BABYSITTING
> Sleep while you work
> Work while you sleep

A young writer who cannot sleep in his tiny apartment because it is too full of books eagerly answers the ad. At first, Julia is furious about the arrangement. However, she is gradually won over by the kind, sensitive young man and his pet owl, Smuggler. Soon she has christened him her "Night Daddy" and the two of them are sharing midnight snacks, training the owl, and tending an exotic tropical plant known as the "Queen of the Night."

II. PREREADING DISCUSSION QUESTIONS

The questions which follow are illustrative of the kinds which teachers can prepare for the purpose of releasing children to reveal how they feel about some of the larger ideas and bigger meanings contained in the book before it is read by the children.

About Aloneness and Loneliness
1. How many reasons can you think of that would explain why a young person would need a *companion?*
2. In choosing playmates, companions, and baby-sitters for their children, why do you think most parents don't do a very good job?
3. Why do you think it is so important to young people to be popular, admired, well-liked?

4. What differences do you think exist between being *alone* and being *lonely?*
5. Most young people like you have a best friend or two who is about the same age. What reasons can you think of that would explain why a young person *doesn't* have a best friend (excluding relatives) who is fifteen or twenty years older?
6. How might you explain the fact that there are some who want to be a person's *best friend* so much that they put up with his/her snubs and meanness?

About One-Parent Homes
7. Why do you think so many people act *differently* toward a young person when they find out that he/she only has one parent?
8. What effects do you think there are on a *one-parent child* when it comes to (1) making friends, (2) going on trips or outings, (3) being happy?

About Secrets
9. How would you describe something that you have done which caused you to feel so ashamed or embarrassed that you *wanted* to be punished in some way so that you could have a clear conscience? Since it is something that only you knew about, how did you go about *punishing yourself?*
10. How many examples can you give that would show whether you agree or disagree with the idea that *"things only become secrets when you begin* talking *about them. Those are the* real *secrets"?*

III. PREREADING ACTIVITIES

The Prereading Activities which follow purpose to elicit *analogous* or *parallel* experiences from the reader's background so that he/she can identify more intensely with the *feelings* of the characters in the book—as they interact with other characters,

183

situations, and events—as he/she reads and finds them familiar because they are but one step removed from the real occurrences in his/her life.

1. **Behavior Modification**

Everyone knows how difficult it is to get rid of a *bad habit,* but what about *good habits?* For example, we are accustomed to eating and sleeping at certain times, following school schedules and routines, reading or writing or studying at regular hours when we feel we are in the best moods for doing these things, and so on. But, what if suddenly your family moved from Hawaii to Delaware and sleeping and eating times were thrown off by almost a half day? You might want to go to Dr. Sy Kem Outt for help.

Dr. Sy Kem Outt is the nation's greatest modifier of *good habits.* That is, he doesn't handle the "common" training jobs such as thumb-sucking, biting fingernails, toilet training, and so forth. Instead he takes on really tough cases! And he has taken on *you* as his assistant in these six new ones:

1. *Training children to smile when very unhappy.*
2. *Training baseball players to say thank you when they strike out.*
3. *Training owls to sleep at night and stay awake by day.*
4. *Training dogs not to growl or bark at strange noises.*
5. *Training teachers to let students do most of the talking in the classroom.*
6. *Training pigeons to retrieve lighted cigarettes carelessly tossed away in woods and forests.*

Dr. Sy Kem Outt has asked you to take on two of the above cases to lighten his load. On the PRESCRIPTION BLANKS below, write out how you would "treat" and thus modify the behavior of your "patients" in these two cases.

184

UPS and DOWNS Clinic
2000 Rainbow's End Drive
CLOUD NINE, N. Y.

Patient's Name_____ Rx No._____

Behavior Problem_____

Treatment Prescription

_____

_____

_____

_____

_____

_____

_____

_____

Dr._____ Date_____

UPS and DOWNS Clinic
2000 Rainbow's End Drive
CLOUD NINE, N. Y.

Patient's Name_____ Rx No._____

Behavior Problem_____

Treatment Prescription

_____

_____

_____

_____

_____

_____

_____

_____

Dr._____ Date_____

2. Evasive Expressions

There are times when people don't wish to tell the truth but, in trying NOT TO TELL A LIE, they try to *evade* the question instead by using various truth-avoiding expressions.

Put yourself in the place of a *truthful truth-evader* in the situations below. After you finish, go back and place an asterisk (*) in front of those that upset you the most when people use them ON YOU.

THE SITUATION	THE EVASIVE EXPRESSION
1. "Mother, can I go to the movies tonight with some of the kids from school?"	_____ _____
2. (To your teacher) "I wasn't feeling very good last night. Is it all right if I hand in my project next week?"	_____ _____
3. "Dad, do you think I could have a couple of dollars?"	_____
4. (To a friend) "How do you like my new jacket?"	_____
5. (To the smartest kid in your class) "Could I please look at your homework?"	_____ _____
6. "I'm really in a jam and could use your help. It'll only take an hour or two of your time."	_____ _____
7. (To a brother or sister) "Could I wear your suit to school tomorrow; it's a special occasion?"	_____ _____

8. *(To your parents) "Terry's
   dog just had puppies and
   she said I could have my
   first pick if you'll agree."*

_____

_____

IV. POSTREADING DISCUSSION QUESTIONS

1. Why do you think Julia had difficulty getting Ulla and her friends to believe that Smuggler and the night daddy really existed?

2. If you heard someone else who had just read this book say that "for an adult, the night daddy is pretty stupid," why would you agree or disagree?

3. On pages 41 and 42 and again on pages 84 and 85 the night daddy's story about the toad and the puddle is told as a way of explaining why there are certain times he can't write. Why do you think your teacher would or would not understand this reasoning if you used it in school?

4. Why do you suppose Julia had so much trouble deciding what to do with her sign:

   PRIVATE PROPERTY!   DO NOT DISTURB!
   TRESPASSING FORBIDDEN!

5. What do you think Julia's reaction to having a baby-sitter at night would have been *even if her mother had discussed it with her first?*

6. How would you try to convince Julia that her opinions of *fathers* are not exactly correct?

7. How might the night daddy's explanation of *proving to himself how free he is by window-shopping* be a good or bad idea for someone like you?

8. *"The hardest thing is to try to console someone. I know that, because I don't believe them when they try to console me."* (P. 135.) Why do you think this is or is not the way that most young people feel when someone tries to sympathize with them and cheer them up? Why would you have expected Julia to feel this way?

9. Why do you think Julia's stubborn ideas of what a *real secret* is (p. 7) and the fact that she doesn't want her classmates to think she *invented* her night daddy (pp. 3 and 149) actually could be the *same* idea?

10. On page 136, Julia says: *"I wouldn't ever want another night daddy, and I'm always going to tell mine the truth."* Since Julia has felt this way almost from the very beginning, why do you think that by the end of the story she still hasn't told him her real name?

V. HELPING CHILDREN TO REVEAL THEIR COMPREHENSION

Name_____

Date_____

1.

Julia's $pending $pree

DIRECTIONS: After her night daddy heard Julia's story about trying to buy some candy with her "valuable" special green stone, he decided to take her on a shopping spree. Knowing Julia as well as you do now, what ONE thing do you think she would buy in each of these departments in the local department store? Fill in her choices.

1. Book Department _____

2. Pet Department _____

3. Household Department _____

4. Men's Department _____

5. Stationery Department _____

6. The Candy Shoppe _____

7. The Garden Center _____

8. Toy and Hobby Department _____

2. Julia's Daddy-Rater

DIRECTIONS: If Julia were comparing her NIGHT DADDY to what she believes all other children's fathers are like, how would she rate them? Using the scale of numbers below circle what you think Julia's rating would be.

RATING SCALE:

Strongly Agree	Agree	Neutral	Disagree	Strongly Disagree
1	2	3	4	5

Items of Comparison	*The Night Daddy*	*All Other Daddies*
1. Nagging about homework	1 2 3 4 5	1 2 3 4 5
2. Rude children are upsetting	1 2 3 4 5	1 2 3 4 5
3. Children's ideas appreciated	1 2 3 4 5	1 2 3 4 5
4. Never too busy to listen	1 2 3 4 5	1 2 3 4 5
5. Pets, flowers, rocks are important	1 2 3 4 5	1 2 3 4 5
6. Showing love and affection	1 2 3 4 5	1 2 3 4 5
7. Having fun	1 2 3 4 5	1 2 3 4 5
8. Making all important decisions	1 2 3 4 5	1 2 3 4 5
9. Always bossing smaller people	1 2 3 4 5	1 2 3 4 5
10. Looking old and harmless	1 2 3 4 5	1 2 3 4 5
11. Telling lies to children	1 2 3 4 5	1 2 3 4 5

3. TV Previews

As you know, at the end of most TV programs, people are shown five or six quick scenes from NEXT WEEK'S show! Since the program next week is going to be Maria Gripe's "The Night Daddy," you have the job of creating the PREVIEWS to televise. Cut out the TV set and paste it on a piece of tagboard or heavy cardboard. Cut "slots" in the TV set on the dotted lines. Cut out the large hole (the channel selector) at the middle of the set. Next, cut out the "TV Tape" strips and glue them together. Decide on the exciting, enticing scenes you wish to televise and draw them in the frames. Under each "shot" write a short caption explaining the scene (for example: SMUGGLER ESCAPES!). Insert the TV tape from the *bottom* of the set and "thread" it (in under/over fashion) until the word "START" appears at the top slot, and the number 1 appears in the channel selector.

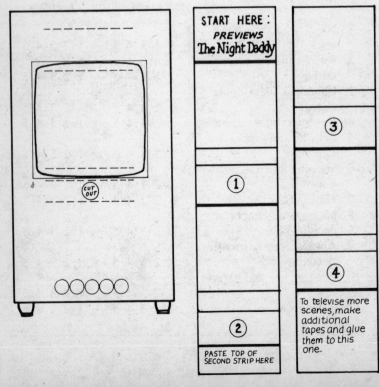

VI. RELATED-TO-READING EXPERIENCES

1. **Julia's Super Gift to the Night Daddy**

For someone interested in rocks, what could be more appropriate than a beautiful CRYSTAL BOUQUET?

Take a small piece of *coal* and place it in a shallow bowl. Then add a supersaturated solution of salt water—enough so that half to two-thirds of the piece of coal is covered. Let stand for several days. Drops of dyes on the piece of coal will cause colorful crystals to form. (Common "dyes" around the house also will work—things such as: merthiolate, laundry bluing, inks, and so forth.) Adding color to the original salt solution will add even more variety in color to your crystal bouquet.

2. **Rock Research**

Do some research on various types of semiprecious stones—including where they are found, how they are formed, what uses (if any) they have. Also, find out what a fossil is and the length of time it takes to form. Begin your own rock collection and learn how to label and store your discoveries. Some starters: Migmatite, hornblende, porphyry, margarite, hematite. Check also: schist, mica, calamine, tourmaline, spinel, and lazalite.

3. **Night Bloomers**

Research and list those plants that bloom at night. Where are they grown and under what conditions?

MYSTERY OF
THE FAT CAT
by FRANK BONHAM

Illustrated by Alvin Smith

I. THE STORY

Everything in Dogtown, including the Boys Club, was run down and beat up. The Health Department wanted to close the club because it was full of rats and cockroaches. But that only meant that the kids like Buddy Williams, Johnny Pastelito, Rich Smith, and Cool Hawkins would be out on the street again with no place to go. They didn't want trouble. They just wanted to raise money to save the old place. Once they started looking, though, things began to pop. Before long, the whole town was in on the search for a very rich and mysterious cat.

II. PREREADING DISCUSSION QUESTIONS

The questions which follow are illustrative of the kinds which teachers can prepare for the purpose of releasing children to reveal how they feel *about some of the larger ideas and bigger meanings contained in the book* before it is read by the children.

About Martyrs
1. A *martyr* is a "person who endures great suffering, pain, or torment frequently as a result of sacrificing something very important to further a cause, belief, or principle." How many situations have you been in where you definitely can state that you played the role of a *martyr*?

2. Frequently a person makes his/her own decision about becoming a *martyr;* however, how many examples can you give that would describe a situation in which a person became a *martyr through no choice of his/her own?*

3. Sometimes *martyrs* are heroes, sometimes hated villains. How many examples can you give of *martyrs* who have been respected and loved as well as despised and hated?

About Pranks and Pranksters

4. What do you think causes some people to get such great kicks from playing practical jokes on others?

5. On Halloween and the first of April people put up with pranks and pranksters which, at any other time, would make them angry. Some would even be considered against the law! How do you feel about the people and the pranks they play on these two days?

6. How many examples can you give that would show the differences between *harmless* and *dangerous* pranks?

About Trespassing and Civil Rights

7. Why do you think people fight so hard for their "rights of privacy"?

8. What do you think a person can do to protect the privacy of his/her property? What can't he/she do?

About Pets and Pests

9. What situation can you imagine that would show how someone's *pet* could be someone else's *pest?*

10. Why do you think such things as mice and rats, worms, bugs, and insects give so many people *creepy,* if not fearful, feelings?

11. What do you think about people who love, care for, and treat a pet better than people? What do you think about pet owners who really act as if their pets were more human than animal?

III. PREREADING ACTIVITIES

The Prereading Activities which follow purpose to elicit *analogous* or *parallel* experiences from the reader's background so that he/she can identify more intensely with the *feelings* of the characters in the book—as they interact with other characters, situations, and events—as he/she reads and finds them familiar because they are but one step removed from the real occurrences in his/her life.

Name_____

Date_____

1. Animal Kooks and Lovers

DIRECTIONS: Some pet owners love their pets so much that they think of them more as HUMANS than animals and, as a result, treat them in ways that a lot of people would call weird or KOOKY! Which of the following would you consider weird, far out, or KOOKY! Put a K on the blank in front. Put an L in front of those you think show nothing more than real love and concern for the pet.

_____1. Leaving a pet horse seven thousand dollars in a will.
_____2. Burying a pet in an animal cemetery.
_____3. Allowing a pet snake the run of the house.
_____4. Having a wedding ceremony for male and female dogs.
_____5. Getting a hair transplant for a cat.
_____6. Having a skin graft for a pet frog.
_____7. Having a dog's tooth cavity filled.
_____8. Buying a gold and silver cage for a pet cricket.
_____9. Painting a pet's nails with fingernail polish.
_____10. Buying expensive jewelry (collars, chains, and so forth) for pets.
_____11. Knitting or sewing coats and scarves for pets.
_____12. Buying a plane ticket for a pet.

2. **When School's Out . . . they ALL begin to shout**

> *DIRECTIONS: For many people your age, the end of the school year is a very happy time because of the FUN-FILLED weeks that are supposed to be ahead. But different people listed below have different FEELINGS (if not worries) about the end of school. On the blanks opposite each person, list as many feelings for him/her as you can think of.*

1. Firemen _____

2. Parents _____

3. Other Relatives _____

4. Policemen _____

5. Wealthy Adults _____

6. Ghetto/Slum Dwellers _____

7. Public Park Employees _____

8. City Officials (mayor, etc.) _____

9. Club Leaders _____

10. Store Owners _____

IV. POSTREADING DISCUSSION QUESTIONS

1. Why do you suppose the Dogtown city officials had such difficulty in reaching a decision about trying to be lenient about keeping the *Oak Street Boys Club* open, or playing it by the book and closing it for health and safety reasons?

2. How can you explain why Dogtown citizens couldn't quite decide whether to be more afraid of the *Oak Street Wildlife* (beetles, rats, roaches, mice) or the other dangerous animal, *known as Boys,* which could crawl from the ruins and roam in the streets in noisy hordes?

3. Ralphie was slow and mentally retarded, but he had what his mother called *Ralphie-magic.* Even though everyone seemed to trust Ralphie, why do you suppose no one seemed to pay much attention to *Ralphie-magic* when he had the solution to the mystery of the cat?

4. Johnny Pastelito, or Little Pie, *seems* to be a good friend, but how can you explain the fact that he always seems either to start the trouble or quickly disappear when trouble comes and leave others holding the bag?

5. On page 34 it says: *"In the Boys Club, it made no difference what a boy had been. Only what he was now, or was trying to be."* Why do you think parents would or would not get along much better with their children if they believed in a statement like that?

6. Why do you suppose it would be difficult to convince many parents to believe that *"any kid would much rather be good than bad"?* (P. 37.)

7. How might you try to argue the point that it took *teamwork* —the *combined talents* of Rich Smith, Cool Hawkins, Little Pie, and Angie, Ralphie, and Buddy Williams—to solve the mystery of Buzzer Atkins?

8. On the very first page of chapter one the author describes Buddy Williams as being clumsy and *"not much good at anything but swimming."* How do Buddy's actions in the story *prove to you that he was pretty clumsy and not much good at anything but swimming?*

1.

WANTED!

You are in the Dogtown Post Office and happen to glance at the WANTED posters. There you see pictured someone from the story you've just read. Who is it most likely to be? What's his/her M.O.?

DEAD OR ALIVE by _____

_____

(Name of Character)

REWARD! $_____

	PROFILE

DRAW HIS/HER PICTURE   R. Thumb PRINT

WANTED FOR: _____

DESCRIPTION: _____

COMPANIONS: _____

LAST SEEN: _____   L. Thumb

WARNINGS: _____   PRINT

IF SEEN OR CAUGHT, CONTACT_____AT_____

HISTORY (if any, of previous evil behavior):_____

_____

_____

Your Name _____   Date_____

2. ¿¿¿**Mystery Match???**

DIRECTIONS: Here is your chance to create a MYSTERY MATCHING GAME for anyone else who reads Mystery of the Fat Cat. *Just fill in the five boxes below with descriptions of the characters in the book which you feel you know the best (one character per box). Then, print their names in the "MYSTERY MATCH BOX" at the bottom of this paper AFTER YOU SCRAMBLE THE LETTERS IN EACH OF THE NAMES FIRST!*

MYSTERY CELEBRITY #1

_____
_____
_____
_____
_____

MYSTERY CELEBRITY #2

_____
_____
_____
_____
_____

MYSTERY CELEBRITY #3

_____
_____
_____
_____
_____

MYSTERY CELEBRITY #4

_____
_____
_____
_____
_____

MYSTERY CELEBRITY #5

_____
_____
_____
_____

Mystery Match Box

1._____

2._____

3._____

4._____

5._____

Cat-Locks

DIRECTIONS: Each of the "locks" below had to be opened in order for the MYSTERY OF THE FAT CAT to be solved. Each of the six "keys" to the "locks" was held by one of the main characters in the story. On each lock, write a brief description of the "secret" which it "unlocks." In the small box on each lock, put the number of the "key" that opened it in the story.

VI. RELATED-TO-READING EXPERIENCES

1. **Zip! Smash! Flash!**
Is Rich Smith's "remote-control" flash really possible? See for yourself. (Reread pp. 94–95.) Using a dart gun or bow and arrow *(the kind of darts and arrows which have the rubber SUCTION CUPS on the ends)* try to hit your own specially drawn target of Buzzer's window from 20 feet. If you are familiar with cameras, and really want to test your skill, try duplicating Rich's experiment at night with a camera. Good shooting!

2. **Lifelong Facts**
What can you find out about the life-spans of some of the most common animals? What can you discover about the longevity of American males? Females? What can you learn of the comparative ages of a fifteen-year-old dog, horse, cat when viewed in terms of HUMAN YEARS? Prepare a chart or graph of your findings.

3. **What's in a Will?**
Find someone in your class or school whose mother or father is an attorney. Ask them to help you draw up a facsimile of a real WILL in which you want to bequeath an animal (turtle, goldfish, rabbit, dog, cat, horse, and so forth) ten thousand dollars! What problems are involved? How must such a WILL be worded? Who else must be involved? You might also ask your attorney if he/she knows of any cases in which money has been left to animals and what the circumstances were.

ARE YOU THERE GOD?
IT'S ME, MARGARET.
by JUDY BLUME

I. THE STORY

Margaret was a bit confused about religion. When she moved from the city to her new home, she didn't know whether to join the Y or the Jewish Community Center. What made matters worse was that, going on twelve, she had plenty to talk over with God. She had a bra but needed to grow a bit to put something in it. Nancy and Gretchen already had got their periods. What was taking her so long? Sometimes she got so frustrated she ignored Him—until the next time when she really needed someone to listen.

II. PREREADING DISCUSSION QUESTIONS

The questions which follow are illustrative of the kinds which teachers can prepare for the purpose of releasing children to reveal how they feel *about some of the larger ideas and bigger meanings contained in the book* before it is read by the children.

About Grandparents
  1. What are some of the most common causes for arguments between the parents of a person your age and their parents (or *your grandparents*)?
  2. Today, parents and their children talk a lot about the generation gap, and most people seem to be able to tell exactly what causes it. But what differences and similarities can you describe in the *gap* which exists between one's *parents* and *grandparents*?

3. Most grandparents try hard to be especially kind and loving to their grandchildren. However, sometimes grandparents' sincere ways to show their love and kindness turn their grandchildren off! What specific examples can you think of that would fit this situation? How can you explain why such misunderstandings between grandparents and their grandchildren could come about?

About Prepuberty Concerns

4. What do you think would be included on an eleven- or twelve-year-old girl's *personal* list showing her ten most important wishes in order of their priority?
5. Very often, a group of about four or five girls who are good friends get together and form a secret club when they are in the sixth or seventh grade in school. What do you think are the purposes for such clubs? What would they do at their meetings? What would they talk about?
6. What are two or three of the biggest growing-up worries girls have? What problems or embarrassment do they cause? Who do you feel is the person(s) you feel you can talk to freely about these worries?

III. PREREADING ACTIVITIES

The Prereading Activities which follow purpose to elicit *analogous* or *parallel* experiences from the reader's background so that he/she can identify more intensely with the *feelings* of the characters in the book—as they interact with other characters, situations, and events—as he/she reads and finds them familiar because they are but one step removed from the real occurrences in his/her daily life.

1. **Preteen Prevaricators**

   DIRECTIONS: There are certain things which some preteen-age girls often lie about (sometimes even to their closest friends). On the blank in front of each statement below, put one of the following letters which you think most girls your age would do:

   A = LIE, 99 percent of the time, even to best friends
   U = USUALLY LIE, except to best friends
   S = SOMETIMES LIE—about 50 percent of the time
   N = NEVER LIES, always tells the truth

   _____How many boys like you?
   _____Do you still wear a training bra?
   _____What religion do you believe in?
   _____How many dates have you had with boys?
   _____Have you begun to menstruate?
   _____Do you like to look at girlie magazines?
   _____Have you ever kissed a boy on the lips?
   _____How often do you look at yourself naked?
   _____Have you ever seen a boy without any clothes on?
   _____Would you go to a party with a boy you can't stand if no one else asked you?

2. Boy-Haters' Test

DIRECTIONS: Many girls your age often say, "I can't stand boys! I hate them!" A few probably mean what they say while most only dislike some of the things boys do or the ways boys act. On the lines in front of each statement below, put a rating mark from 0 to 5 (0 = you love this quality in a boy; 5 = you absolutely detest this in a boy). After you finish the book, you will be able to find out whether or not you really are a BOY HATER!

1. _____Boys who stand around and grin and stare at you all the time as if you were naked.
2. _____Boys who always hang around with two or three other boys and make smart remarks whenever a girl passes by.
3. _____Boys who play practical jokes.
4. _____Boys who are good in their schoolwork and show it!
5. _____Boys who use foul and obscene language.
6. _____Boys who brag about how crazy all the girls are over them.
7. _____Boys who are tough, top athletic stars and play hard to get.
8. _____Boys who let other boys run all over them.
9. _____Boys who brag about what they do with girls on a date.
10. _____Boys who let their parents run their lives.
11. _____Boys who dress mod.
12. _____Boys who don't believe in Women's Lib.
13. _____A boy who is your best friend's brother.
14. _____Boys who are polite, well-mannered.
15. _____Boys who aren't afraid to talk back to any adult.

IV. POSTREADING DISCUSSION QUESTIONS

1. What do you think are the possible reasons behind Mr. and Mrs. Simon's decision to raise Margaret as neither Christian nor Jew?

2. On page 133, Margaret's mother asked the Hutchinses (her parents) to stop talking about religion: *"Please . . . Margaret could just as easily be Jewish. Don't you see—if you keep this up you're going to spoil everything."* What do you think Margaret's mother was worried about?

3. Some readers have thought that the generation gap between Margaret's parents and *their* parents (her three grandparents) was greater than the generation gap between Margaret and her mother and father. Why do you think such a belief might be true?

4. What reasons can you give that might explain why Margaret confided in and sought information from the girls in the Four PTS (Pre-Teen Sensations) secret club rather than from her own mother?

5. Nancy, Janie, Gretchen, and Margaret all seemed to have very strong reasons for disliking Laura Danker. Now that you know more about Laura, how would you argue with the members of the Four PTS and their feelings toward Laura Danker?

6. A lot of people, if they were to learn that the three main rules of the Four PTS Club concerned bras, boys, and menstruation, would think that this is a silly, freakish way for normal girls to spend their time. Tell why you would or would not agree with people who would criticize the purposes these four girls have for their secret club.

7. Why do you think some of the girls in the club lied about getting their periods? Why do you think Margaret was so shocked when she found this out?

V. HELPING CHILDREN TO REVEAL
THEIR COMPREHENSION

Name_____

Date_____

1.

ARE YOU THERE, MARGARET?
IT'S ME, GOD!

If Margaret Ann Simon had received answers to her prayers, what do you think they might have been?

"Are you there God? It's me, Margaret. We're moving today. I'm so scared, God. I've never lived anywhere but here. Suppose I hate my new school? Suppose everybody there hates me? Please help me, God. Don't let New Jersey be too horrible. Thank you."

"Are you there God? It's me, Margaret. I just told my mother I want a bra. Please help me grow, God. You know where. I want to be like everyone else. You know, God, my new friends all belong to the Y or the Jewish Community Center. Which way am I supposed to go? I don't know what you want me to do about that."

"Are you there God? It's me, Margaret. Gretchen, my friend, got her period. I'm so jealous, God. I hate myself for being so jealous, but I am. I wish you'd help me a little. Nancy's sure she's going to get it soon, too. And if I'm last I don't know what I'll do. Oh please, God. I just want to be normal."

2. Moody Margaret

As with most people, Margaret Ann Simon has different feelings about different people she comes into contact with throughout the story. These moods are plain enough by looking at the expressions on Margaret's faces below. But, what is Margaret saying to or about the people? Put words into Moody Margaret's mouth!

Norman Fishbein, _____

Philip Leroy, _____

Grandma and Grandpa Hutchins, _____
_____
_____
_____
_____

(Grandma) Sylvia, _____
_____
_____
_____
_____
_____

Laura Danker, _____
_____
_____
_____
_____
_____

Mother, _____
_____
_____
_____

Nancy, _____
_____
_____
_____

Mr. Benedict, _____
_____
_____
_____

3. **Boy-Haters' Test—Part II**

DIRECTIONS: Using the "Boy-Haters' Test" (p. 204), enter the ratings for each item the way you believe Margaret Ann Simon would have responded to them. Now add all the ratings together and compare the results on the scale below:

    0 to 16 = You must still be in your crib!
16 to 31 = You could use some lessons in being choosy.
31 to 40 = You've got to be kidding!
41 to 56 = OK, but Women's Lib won't like it.
57 to 68 = Boys you can do without!
69 to 73 = Boys are lousy, stupid, horrid, despicable monsters!
74 to 75 = A boy hater, 100 percent.

VI. RELATED-TO-READING EXPERIENCES

1. Many people, even today, still feel that it is unwise for people of different religions, different races, different cultures or cultural backgrounds to marry. Perhaps this is why there was so much friction between Margaret's grandparents and her parents. Perhaps this is why Margaret was so frustrated and unhappy. What can you find out about the way other Jewish-Christian parents have solved the problem about what religion to expose their children to? To what extent (if any) were the grandparents involved?

2. The PTS club had three rules and a meeting date, but little else. If they had written a Constitution, what would it have said? If they had planned a regular "Saturday Afternoon Safari" where would they have gone and what would they have done that would fit into the purposes of the club?

3. Most girls are shown a special movie about menstruation in school. If you have not yet seen such a film, make a list of the six most important questions you would like to have answered. If you have seen it, make a list of questions or complaints you have about the film and the facts you wanted but did not receive.

THEN AGAIN, MAYBE I WON'T
by JUDY BLUME

I. THE STORY

Ever since his father got rich from his invention and the family moved from Jersey City to a posh community on Long Island, thirteen-year-old Tony Miglione had had nothing but problems. There was his friend Joel, who Tony knew was a shoplifter. And there was Joel's sixteen-year-old sister, Lisa, who got undressed every night without pulling down her shades. Having a lot of money brought problems, too. The new maid exiled Grandma from the kitchen, and Tony's mother was becoming a social-climbing phony. On top of all that, there were the growing-up problems that all boys must face. And if his parents and friends knew what Tony thought about the whole business, they'd probably flip.

II. PREREADING DISCUSSION QUESTIONS

The questions which follow are illustrative of the kinds which teachers can prepare for the purpose of releasing children to reveal how they feel about some of the larger ideas and bigger meanings contained in the book before it is read by the children.

About Generations and Gaps
1. Why do you think so many parents are either very "clumsy" or else no help at all when they try to have personal talks with their children about sex drives or the normal, maturing, growth changes and happenings of the body as one reaches puberty?

2. What reasons can you think of that cause some people to believe that *no two families can live under the same roof?*

3. When parents say, *". ... But we're doing all of this for you so that you'll have a better and easier life than we had when we were growing up!"* many children seem to become more angry rather than more appreciative. How can you try to explain this?

4. How would you expect the disagreements between a child and his/her parents to be different in poor or average income families from those of a child and his/her parents who are wealthy? How do you believe they might be exactly the same?

About Friendship

5. Why do you think most people feel that ratting or telling on a best friend for cheating in school or stealing is so difficult to do, or even something one shouldn't do?

6. When some of your closest friends *dare* you to do something you don't feel is right even though they insist that it is a harmless prank, why is the decision you have to make such a difficult one?

7. What reasons can you give that might explain why it is so important to some parents to approve or disapprove of their children's friends?

About Affluence and Materialism

8. What do you believe are some of the main reasons why children and their parents disagree so much about money?

9. Nearly everyone has known someone (either a schoolmate or an adult) who has tried to have the same things and to act like someone else whom they believe is very upstanding, proper, and admired. Why would you agree or disagree with those who would call such people phonies?

10. When trying to plead with one's parents by using such arguments as: *"But all the other kids at school have one!"* or, *"Everyone else does; why can't I?"* most young people admit that this only angers parents more and makes them more stubborn. What kinds of examples could you give to prove that this is or is not so?

III. PREREADING ACTIVITIES

The Prereading Activities which follow purpose to elicit *analogous* or *parallel* experiences from the reader's background so that he/she can identify more intensely with the *feelings* of the characters in the book—as they interact with other characters, situations, and events—as he/she reads and finds them familiar because they are but one step removed from the real occurrences in his/her life.

1. **Embarrassing Moments**

DIRECTIONS: The face below could be the face of either one of the Blush Twins—Billy or Barbe Blush!—whichever you prefer. Notice that there is a grid or a series of vertical and horizontal lines which break the face up into small areas (most of which are squares) including the ears. There are sixty-eight of these areas in all.

Suppose the face were yours and YOU were caught doing each of the twelve things listed below! When caught in EMBARRASSING SITUATIONS, most people blush. If, for example, after reading #1, you feel you would NOT feel embarrassed at all IF YOU WERE CAUGHT, do nothing and go on to #2. But (on a scale of 1 to 5) color RED those areas to show the AMOUNT OF EMBARRASSMENT you would feel: 1 if very little, 5 if you believe you would feel absolutely mortified for each of the situations.

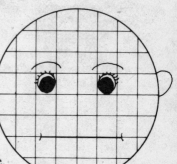

IF I WERE CAUGHT . . .
1. Smoking.
2. Cheating in school.
3. Drinking beer or liquor.
4. Lying to someone close to me.
5. Shoplifting.
6. Masturbating.
7. Stealing small change parents
        leave around the house.
8. Looking at nudie pictures.
9. Calling people on the telephone and
        making them feel stupid or foolish.
10. Spying on someone as he/she undresses.
11. Marking the sexy parts of books and magazines
        and trading them with friends.
12. Snooping into the personal belongings of some
        member of my family.

IV. POSTREADING DISCUSSION QUESTIONS

1. Tony Miglione was so upset over Joel's shoplifting that he became sick; yet it never bothered him when his brother, Ralph, a teacher who didn't have much money, seemed to have no trouble "obtaining" all the school supplies Tony needed! What reasons can you give that might explain this apparent contradiction?

2. On pages 80–81 Tony wonders why his brother Ralph has become so different and guesses that it might be due to the fact that he became a father for the first time. What kinds of things would you say to Tony which might help him understand why Ralph seems to be different?

3. When Tony learned that his brother was going to join his father in the "Electrical Cartridge" business, he became uptight because he felt Ralph was selling out! What do you think he meant? Why do you think it bothered him so much?

4. On page 130, Tony said that both he and his grandma have a lot in common: *"We're both outsiders in our own home."* How would you describe why he felt this way?

5. As a result of Mr. Miglione's invention, the family suddenly became quite wealthy. Since none of them has ever had *experience in being rich,* a number of *insensitive* things were said and done, especially by Mrs. Miglione. How would you argue against or in favor of her reasons for (a) giving Tony an allowance, (b) getting a second car, and (c) her keeping Maxine on as cook and housekeeper?

6. Tony was terribly embarrassed as well as fearful that people would learn of his wet dreams or notice his uncontrollable erections when they occurred at the most inopportune times. What reasons can you give that would explain Tony's haunting guilt feelings about these normal and natural body functions that occur in all maturing, healthy young boys?

7. Everyone laughed (p. 80) when Tony said, *"What's so great about being rich?"* Since they've only been wealthy for about a year, how can you account for these two *different* positions about wealth in the family?

8. While the entire family was gathered at the new Miglione home in Rosemont for Thanksgiving dinner, Tony's Aunt Rose, in referring to her mother (Tony's grandmother), said: *"Mama's lucky to be able to spend her last years in such luxury."* And later they all decided that the reason Grandma "took to her room" was plain old age. Tony said he knew better, but didn't say anything. Why do you think everyone else believed the way they did about Grandma locking herself in her room?

9. Tony appears to be a pretty honest and trustworthy person and yet (a) *he lied to Lisa when he told her that cigarette smoking caused her grandmother to have cancer of the larynx, (b) he continued his father's lie by covering up for him when Mr. Dalto (his father's ex-boss) called to find out if his "sick" father was feeling better, and (c) many people would claim he was lying by keeping silent as he so often did because he didn't want "any trouble."* Why would you agree or disagree with Tony's philosophy (p. 62) when he says to himself: *"Sometimes it's better to tell a little lie than to tell the truth and have everybody hate you."*?

10. On page 158, Tony was thinking of Joel Hoober when he asked himself: *"What is a friend, anyway?"* How do you think Tony might have answered himself?

11. Joel Hoober was finally caught shoplifting! What are your honest opinions about the fairness of his punishment?

V. HELPING CHILDREN TO REVEAL
THEIR COMPREHENSION

Name_____

Date_____

BUTTON, BUTTON . . .
Who's Got the Button?

DIRECTIONS: Design and color the "BUTTONS" below so that they express the PERSONALITIES, BELIEFS, and/or ATTITUDES of the people in the story, Then Again, Maybe I Won't. *Be sure to put their names on the lines under each BUTTON. You may want to refresh your memory by reviewing the names of some of the major characters:*

Tony Miglione, Ralph Miglione, Grandma, Carmella Miglione (Tony's mother), Vic Miglione (Tony's father), Joel Hoober, "Corky" Kathryn Thomas, Vinnie, Angie, Maxine, Ted Gibbons, J. W. Fullerbach.

_____
(Name of Character)

_____
(Name of Character)

_____
(Name of Character)

_____
(Name of Character)

_____
(Name of Character)

_____
(Name of Character)

_____
(Name of Character)

2.

Name_____

Date_____

DIRECTIONS: Heaven forbid, but you have just been acclaimed the nation's top GRAFFITI ARTIST! And now that you've just finished reading Then Again, Maybe I Won't, *you've found a whole case of aerosol spray paint in a variety of colors. To top it all off, you've discovered four unused roadside billboards that every member in your family is sure to see as they drive to the cemetery on Veterans Day to visit Vinnie's grave. Since you and Tony Miglione think and feel alike, there are things about the move to Rosemont from Jersey City that upset you! You want to get the COMMUNIQUES or messages across to them ANONYMOUSLY; so on your new red, ten-speed, Schwinn bicycle and your cans of spray paint, you ride to each of the billboards and GRIPE in GRAFFITI!*

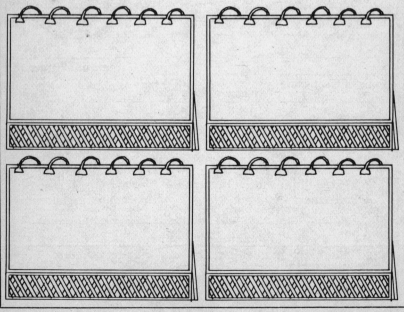

218

8.

Name_____

Date_____

DIRECTIONS: As you know, Grandma refused even to try to learn to speak after her operation for cancer of the larynx; therefore, whenever she had something to say, she wrote notes. Now that you've become so well acquainted with Grandma and the rest of the Miglione family, you probably have a very good idea what Grandma MIGHT HAVE WRITTEN ON THE MEMOS below. What do you think her feelings were? What would she have said?

● MEMO ●

To: _____
Re: About Housekeepers
   and Cooks

_____
_____
_____
_____

● MEMO ●

To _____
Re: About Money and
   Wealth

_____
_____
_____
_____

● MEMO ●

To _____
Re: About Moving to
   Rosemont

_____
_____
_____
_____
_____

● MEMO ●

To _____
Re: About George & Diane
   Hoober, the neighbors

_____
_____
_____
_____

Name_____

Date_____

1.

YOU CAN READ THIS MESSAGE!

(Then Again, Maybe You Can't!)

DIRECTIONS: Read each of the "EITHER-OR" statements below. Make up your mind which of the TWO possible answers is the correct one and follow the directions carefully by putting the designated letters of the alphabet on the lines above the numerals in the long "box" at the right.→

1. Is the "E" pronounced in Miglione? If it isn't, put an S on the lines numbered 13, 17, 25, and 28. If it is pronounced, put the letter D on these lines. (See p. 38.)

2. If Grandma got cancer of the larynx from smoking cigarettes, put the letter U on lines 6, 9, 15, and 27. If not, put the letter I on these lines. (See p. 151.)

3. Tony was pleased that his brother Ralph decided to stop teaching and go in business with his father. If this is TRUE, put an M on lines numbered 2, 10, and 20. If this statement is FALSE, put an O on these lines. (See p. 128.)

```
___  ___  ___  ___  ___  ___  ___  ___  ___  ___  ___
 1    2    3    4    5    6    7    8    9   10   11
```

12 |
13 |
14 |

4. Whenever Diane Hoober felt it was too much trouble to pronounce a person's "funny" name, she gave him/her a nickname. So, instead of calling Mrs. Miglione "Carmella," she renamed her Carol! If this made Tony happy, put a B on lines 8, 19, and 26. If he was angry and upset, put an L on these lines. (See p. 107.)

15 |
16 |
17 |

5. If Tony made the winning basket for the big game against the First Methodist Youth Group, put a D on lines numbered 1 and 18; if he didn't make the winning basket, put a T on those lines. (See p. 114.)

18 |
19 |

6. Tony was allowed to decide whether or not he wanted to continue taking piano lessons. If this is TRUE, put an N on lines 3 and 11. If it is FALSE, put a U on these lines. (See p. 110.)

20 |
21 |

7. Even though they had someone to cook the meals (Maxine), Mrs. Miglione still had to cook Grandma's meals. If this is TRUE, put an E on lines 12 and 22; if FALSE, put an M on these lines. (See p. 66.)

22 |
23 |

8. If Ralph and Angie decided to buy a house and move to Rosemont, put the letter A on lines 24 and 29. If they decided to stay in Queens, put the letter B on these lines. (See p. 151.)

24 |
25 |

9. Now . . . can you read the message? Here's a hint: *It's about the two people involved in a one-sided love affair!* If you still can't read it, put the letter Y on line 4, M on line 5, G on line 7, F on line 14, R on line 16, V on line 21, and W on line 23. If it still makes no sense, check your answers by rereading the page of the book indicated after each.

26 |
27 |
28 |
29 |

2. **The Midas Touch**

DIRECTIONS: As you know, King Midas was granted his wish and everything he touched afterward, including his daughter, turned to GOLD! However fanciful, there are, in today's real world, real people with "Midas Wishes" and once in a while such wishes come true. People win lotteries, for example, or inherit a fortune, or strike it rich as Mr. Miglione did with his invention. When sudden wealth comes to people who have never been rich, things change quickly and drastically. Money brings them a lot of happiness, but along with the happiness— almost always—comes the inevitable sadness of the CURSE OF THE MIDAS TOUCH.

In the column on the left, there are listed a lot of happy and wonderful things that can happen to change a family's way of living as a result of suddenly becoming wealthy. In the right-hand column, write in what you believe could become of the "MIDAS TOUCH" kinds of "CURSES" that one should expect or at least be on the lookout for.

Advantages of Sudden Wealth	The King Midas Touch
1. A new home in the suburbs!	_____
	_____

222

Advantages of Sudden Wealth	The King Midas Touch
2. Getting an allowance instead of having to work at part-time jobs!	
3. A chance to go to the best school in the country!	
4. Being able to afford to belong to expensive clubs!	
5. Receiving expensive gifts of things one's always wanted on birthdays and at holidays!	
6. The financial ability to employ gardeners, maids, housekeepers, cooks, etc.!	
7. Buying the finest clothes of the latest fashions!	
8. Becoming a two-car family —new and prestigious models!	

ISLAND OF THE BLUE DOLPHINS

by SCOTT O'DELL

I. THE STORY

In the Pacific there is an island that looks like a big fish sunning itself in the sea. Around it, blue dolphins swim, otters play, and sea elephants and seabirds abound. Once, Indians also lived on the island. And when they left and sailed to the east, one young girl was left behind.

This is the story of Karana, the Indian girl who lived alone for years on the Island of the Blue Dolphins. Year after year, she watched one season pass into another and waited for a ship to take her away. But while she waited, she kept herself alive by building shelter, making weapons, finding food, and fighting her enemies, the wild dogs. It is not only an unusual adventure of survival, but also a tale of natural beauty and personal discovery.

II. PREREADING DISCUSSION QUESTIONS

The questions which follow are illustrative of the kinds which teachers can prepare for the purpose of releasing children to reveal how they feel *about some of the larger ideas and bigger meanings contained in the book* before it is read by the children.

About Skill Deficiency
1. What emergency or unusual situation have you been in where you needed a simple, common skill in order to cope with the problem and then discovered you had absolutely no idea about where to begin?

2. Young people learn how to do certain things from many different *teachers*—friends, parents, brothers and sisters, Scout leaders, and schoolteachers, for example. What do most young people learn *at home?*

3. In what situation have you found yourself where all of your friends knew how to do something and you were embarrassed because you did not?

4. One of the important goals of those fighting for women's rights is to neutralize, if not turn around, the kind of thinking that classifies jobs and skills into rigid male-female categories. As a result of this thinking in the past, there are still a number of simple, everyday skills which girls and boys have never been taught. (Boys sewing on a button, girls repairing a bicycle chain, for example.) How many different, common "boy-girl deficiencies" can you list? What do you think is being done to prevent such categorizations in future generations?

About the Rights of Animals

5. What opinions do you have about the often-argued statement that *no animal should be hunted, trapped, and/or killed?*

6. Some people believe that it's all right to make *any* animal a pet, even wild animals. Others say that this is very cruel. What are your opinions?

III. PREREADING ACTIVITIES

The Prereading Activities which follow purpose to elicit *analogous* or *parallel* experiences from the reader's background so that he/she can identify more intensely with the *feelings* of the characters in the book—as they interact with other characters, situations, and events—as he/she reads and finds them familiar because they are but one step removed from the real occurrences in his/her daily life.

1. Primitive Priorities

The way you live today, you might have little or no use for the items listed below. But . . . SUPPOSE YOU were marooned on an island or lost in a jungle wilderness where the climate is warm, plenty of food and water available, and no other human inhabitants (but an abundance of wild animals). In front of each item below, place a 1, 2, 3, and so forth to put them in the PRIORITY ORDER you feel necessary for you to stay alive!

___a raft or canoe

___weapons (spear, bow and arrow)

___some dishes

___a knife (made of bone or shell)

___food and water

___a flintstone

___a pet

___some firewood

___some clothes

___a hut or cabin

___a fence

___an SOS signal

___a fishhook and line

(After you finish the story, RENUMBER these items the way Karana gave them her priority. In what ways were your priorities alike? Why did you differ?)

Antitradition Sensor

DIRECTIONS: The actions of many people are governed by tradition and superstition. Opposite each statement below, put an X in the appropriate box if you believe this is the way MOST PEOPLE BELIEVED BEFORE 1950. or if it is the way you believe MOST PEOPLE BELIEVED AFTER 1950. In the third column marked "B. D." (Blue Dolphin), do nothing until after you've finished the story. Then, mark each statement to show how you think the people of the Island of the Blue Dolphins would have believed.

	BEFORE 1950	AFTER 1950	B. D.
1. Once a wild animal, always a wild animal.			
2. Women should have nothing to do with making or using weapons.			
3. Never make an agreement with someone you don't trust.			
4. Girls are not interested in the same things that boys like to do.			
5. Boys can survive better than girls for a long period of time if circumstances force them to live harmoniously with only those things nature has to offer.			
6. Even if one has to lose his/her life, it is better to fight for one's ideas and property than to give in to a more powerful enemy.			
7. If one believes in superstition, then bad or evil things will happen if he/she goes against these beliefs.			

IV. POSTREADING DISCUSSION QUESTIONS

1. On the Island of the Blue Dolphins, women were not allowed to make weapons. According to superstition, the earth would tremble, the sea would rise over the island, and/or the weapons would break. In the story, Karana violated the law and two of these superstitious predictions came true. How might such a natural coincidence reinforce superstitious people's beliefs? How do you think Karana's life might have been different if she had been superstitious?

2. There is a saying: *"For every loss there is a gain; for every gain there is a loss."* How would you agree or disagree with this saying if you use Karana's life on the island as the basis for your judgment?

3. At first, Karana was very reluctant about becoming friends with Tutok. How then can you explain why they finally became friends?

4. Toward the end of the story (p. 156), Karana said that she would never kill another dog! Why do you think her attitudes changed so drastically?

5. Many antifeminists (people who are against the Women's Liberation Movement) say that females are the weaker sex. Basing your arguments on Karana's experiences in the Island of the Blue Dolphins, discuss why you would agree or disagree with the idea that females are the weaker sex.

V. HELPING CHILDREN TO REVEAL
THEIR COMPREHENSION

1. **Citation Servers**

   DIRECTIONS: The American Society for the Prevention of Cruelty to Animals (ASPCA) has sent you to the Island of the Blue Dolphins to find out how the animals are treated. You have been commissioned with the power to hand out citations to people for both kind and cruel deeds to animals. Fill in the following CITATIONS, awarding a "BLESS YOU" Citation for kind deeds and a "CURSE YOU" Citation for cruel deeds to animals.

BLESS YOU

Nature of the Deed: _____

_____

_____

Person Committing Deed: ___

_____

_____

Reasons for Committing the Deed: _____

_____

_____

_____

CURSE YOU

Nature of the Deed: _____

_____

_____

Person Committing Deed: ___

_____

_____

Reasons for Committing the Deed: _____

_____

_____

_____

2. Tombstone Talent

DIRECTIONS: Suppose that now, many years after the story concluded, the bodies of the main characters in the story have been shipped back to the Island of the Blue Dolphins for proper burials in their own land. The only problem is that there was no one around to write the appropriate EPITAPHS on the tombstones, so, up to now, they remain blank.

Since you know the characters best, you have been commissioned by Mr. Heeza Gravely to go to the Island of the Blue Dolphins to complete the job GRAVELY TOMBSTONES, INC., promised would be done. On each of the tombstones below, write a brief epitaph for each of the characters—something appropriate, descriptive, and identifying (and perhaps creatively clever, too!) that will also reveal your talent as the World's Best Tombstone Chiseler!

RAMO

_____
_____
_____
_____
_____
_____

Rest in Peace

KARANA

_____
_____
_____
_____
_____
_____

Rest in Peace

TUTOK

_____

_____

_____

_____

_____

_____

Rest in Peace

CAPTAIN ORLOV

_____

_____

_____

_____

_____

Rest in Peace

CHIEF CHOWIG

_____

_____

_____

_____

_____

_____

Rest in Peace

RONTU

_____

_____

_____

_____

_____

_____

Rest in Peace

3. Plenipotentiary

DIRECTIONS: There were serious flaws in the agreement between Chief Chowig and Captain Orlov. These flaws led to destruction and, subsequently, to the mass migration of the remainder of the island people. As Head of "Small Nation Affairs" you are sent by the United Nations to act as mediator. Draw up a trade agreement that you would consider fair to both sides.

Trade Agreement

for: The Hunting of Otters
on: The Island of the Blue Dolphins

* * *

I, Chief Chowig, shall agree to:

_____

_____

_____

_____

_____

_____

_____

I, Captain Orlov, shall agree to:

_____

_____

_____

_____

_____

_____

I,_____, representing The United Nations on Small Nation Affairs, do hereby swear and attest that both sides have entered into the above mutually binding agreement on this_____ day of_____, _____.

U.N.

VI. RELATED-TO-READING EXPERIENCES

1. You have been contracted to do a movie for Dolphin Brothers Studio about natural disasters on the Island of the Blue Dolphins. Write a screenplay describing the earthquake and tidal wave (chap. 27). Include comparisons of how the island was before, during, and after the disasters. Be sure, also, to indicate when you would use aerial, close-up, panoramic, freeze, and slow-motion shots. Select appropriate music to accompany the film (for example, in *2001: A Space Odyssey,* Strauss music is used).

2. The United Nations Security Council has selected you to help the inhabitants of the Island of the Blue Dolphins battle the Aleuts in chapter six. Your commanding officer, General Snihplod (born and raised as an Aleut until he found more peaceful and human ways of living), asks you for a report which includes these things:

    (a) A detailed map of the island

    (b) Using the resources of the island, *only,* yourself, and the natives—list:

        (1) possible fortifications

        (2) a strategy to win the battle

        (3) all the possible "Do It Yourself" weapons that can be made on the island.

Supply General Snihplod with the report he needs to win!

THE YEAR OF THE THREE-LEGGED DEER

by ETH CLIFFORD

Illustrated by Richard Cuffari

I. THE STORY

Tecumseh is dead, the Indian wars are over, and life for trader Jesse Benton, his Lenni Lenape wife, and his two children, Takawsu and Chilili, seems to promise nothing but happiness. Thus, the spring of 1819 along the Indiana frontier begins peaceably enough when fourteen-year-old Takawsu brings home a mutilated fawn to his sister, who raises it with the help of her pet wolf. And the prospects for the future seem even better when Takawsu's father purchases the freedom of Sakkaape, an educated black slave who has saved the boy's life. Then the bitter racial hatred of a few white men shatters the family's happiness with terrible suddenness. An attempt to kidnap and reenslave Sakkaape leads to the massacre of a peaceful band of Indians, an act that almost sets the frontier ablaze in another Indian war and separates Jesse Benton from his family forever.

II. PREREADING DISCUSSION QUESTIONS

The questions which follow are illustrative of the kinds which teachers can prepare for the purpose of releasing children to reveal how they feel about some of the larger ideas and bigger meanings contained in the book before it is read by the children.

About Prejudice and Racial Hatred

1. Some children have mothers and fathers of different racial groups or with different religious faiths. What do you think might be some of the problems the *children* growing up in such families might face?

2. At one time in our country, only white men were protected by the government and its laws. How do you think a nonwhite person your age might have felt about his/her future and his/her relationships with white children?

3. In recent times we have heard much about a change in *venue,* that is, the place where a trial is held and from which the jury is drawn. In such instances, the defendants and their attorneys feel that a fair trial is impossible. Even though granting a change in venue is not too common today, it was almost unheard of prior to the 1900s. How do you think this could have contributed to the bitter and long-lasting prejudice and hatred between minority groups (whether racial, religious, or place of birth) and a larger, different, homogeneous community where the vast majority looked alike and held values and beliefs and customs that were the same?

4. Very often, when one does not conform to customs of the community in which he/she lives (such as washing clothes on Sunday, or fencing in his/her property), he/she is subject to gossip, ridicule, and not too infrequently ostracized from many social and community gatherings. Why do you suppose the *children* of such parents seem to have the hardest time adjusting and being happy in such a community?

About Animals

5. Some people have a way with animals. If you saw or talked with such a person what are some of the things you would notice about him/her that would be different from people who don't have this special touch?

6. Some animals are supposed to be natural enemies! For example, it is not unusual to hear people say, *"They fight like cats and dogs!"* Cats and dogs are *supposed* to be *natural enemies* and yet, many people who have *both* a cat and a dog as a pet will tell you they live amiably together. What are some other animals you think are "natural enemies"? How long a list can you make? How would you try to verify your list?

7. Some people think that any wild animal can be trained to be a good pet for humans; yet there are others who claim that there are some such animals who will never accept, love, and trust human beings. What animals do you know about, or have heard about, that would seem to you as the most *unlikely* to raise as a pet?

About Hindsight and Foresight

8. Think about the things you've done this past week. What situations were you in that caused you to say to yourself (or to someone else):

(a) If only I hadn't_____, then_____!
(b) If I had just_____, then_____!
(c) I should have known that_____, because_____!
(d) How dumb can I be? I knew all along that_____!

9. What's one of the most serious things you've ever been involved in in which you could say that your hindsight is better than your foresight?

III. PREREADING ACTIVITIES

The Prereading Activities which follow purpose to elicit *analogous* or *parallel* experiences from the reader's background so that he/she can identify more intensely with the *feelings* of the characters in the book—as they interact with other characters, situations, and events—as he/she reads and finds them familiar because they are but one step removed from the real occurrences in his/her life.

1. **Paradox or Prejudice?**

Many people who admit they have prejudices will argue that they believe as they do because *it is in the best interests of all the people.* As paradoxical as it may seem, certain kinds of segregation and discrimination might appear to you to be "right" and "proper." Listed below are some examples. On the blank in front of each put an R if *you* think the idea is RIGHT or "in the best interests of all (or most) of the people." Put a W if *you* think the idea is WRONG or unfair.

_____1. *No Smoking* sections on planes, trains, and busses.

_____2. *No Pets Allowed* rules of motels and hotels.

_____3. Apartment owners who will not rent to people who have young children.

_____4. Schools that believe everyone should read *before* second grade.

_____5. Only a person born in the United States should be President.

_____6. Clubs that are "For Blacks Only!"

_____7. Not permitting shops and department stores to do business on Sundays (blue laws).

_____8. Refusing to hire a man who wears shoulder-length hair and high heels on his shoes.

_____9. Paying a man a higher salary than a woman for doing the *same* job.

_____10. Places of business that refuse to let you in unless you are wearing shoes.

_____11. Companies who won't issue credit cards to unmarried women.

_____12. Businesses that make people stop working when they reach a certain age (usually sixty-five).

IV. POSTREADING DISCUSSION QUESTIONS

1. At the Fourth of July celebration, Jesse Benton read from the *Declaration of Independence* (p. 79). What do you think Sakkaape was thinking and feeling as he listened?

2. What do you think are some of the reasons that caused Mekinges to decide to move on with the Lenni Lenape?

3. Suppose Chilili had not met her tragic death. Why do you think this would or would not have changed Mekinges' decision to go with her tribe and Jesse's decision to remain behind?

4. What reasons can you give that might explain why Jesse Benton decided to stay behind and let his wife, son, and Sakkaape move on to the new Indian territory?

5. What can you tell about Judge Harvey Sweetz that made you feel that the trial would or would not be a fair one?

6. How many qualities can you list that might explain why the people elected Jesse Benton a senator?

7. What possible reasons can you think of that might explain how Stone Eater became such a bitter, cruel man?

8. How would you describe your feelings toward the Indians during the trial of Noble Loomis and again as Colonel Barron and Chief Skoligiso finalized the agreement that sent the Lenni Lenape in search of new homeland west of the Mississippi?

9. On page 157, Skoligiso bitterly questions Colonel Barron:
   "And did he pay for the air we breathe, the
   clouds above our heads, the sun in the sky,
   the rain that falls from the heavens?"

It is doubtful, even if he had had a chance to reply, that Colonel Barron could have come up with any kind of sensible answer to Skoligiso's inquiry. But suppose you had been in the colonel's place, representing the President of the United States. How might you have tried to respond to the chief's anguish?

V. HELPING CHILDREN TO REVEAL
THEIR COMPREHENSION

1. **Totem of Events Calendar:** October 1819–October 1820
   Suppose the TOTEM POLE below listed—from bottom to top—the sequence of major events and the people in-

volved for the year of the three-legged deer, a permanent record of an arresting moment of history for future generations to read. What events and whose names would you "carve" into the TOTEM CALENDAR under the headings provided for you by Takawsu?

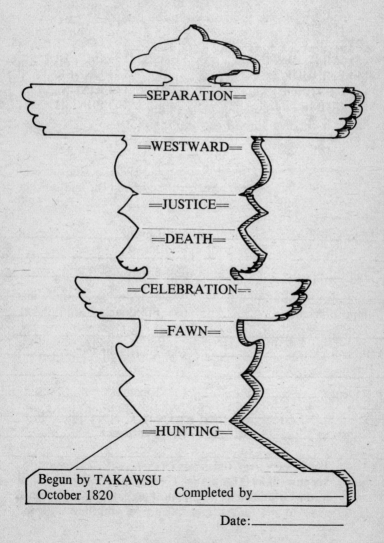

=SEPARATION=

=WESTWARD=

=JUSTICE=

=DEATH=

=CELEBRATION=

=FAWN=

=HUNTING=

Begun by TAKAWSU
October 1820   Completed by_____

Date:_____

2. Balancing Good and Evil in Bentonville

evil	good
(1) HATE	(1) LOVE
(2) GUILT	(2) FORGIVENESS
(3) IMPRISONMENT	(3) FREEDOM
(4) PREJUDICE	(4) UNDERSTANDING
(5) REVENGE	(5) KINDNESS
(6) CRIME	(6) PUNISHMENT

JUSTICE

(1) Hate: _____

(2) Guilt: _____

(3) Imprisonment: _____

(4) Prejudice: _____

(5) Revenge: _____

(6) Crime: _____

(1) Love: _____

(2) Forgiveness: _____

(3) Freedom: _____

(4) Understanding: _____

(5) Kindness: _____

(6) Punishment: _____

While this story, *The Year of the Three-Legged Deer,* is full of many evildoers, injustices, and almost unbearably sad events, there seems to be, for each, a balance of unbelievably good happenings, justice, and right-doers. For each of the six "evils" listed above, briefly fill in the blanks with the person, act, place, and/or event which you believe from the story is best associated with, for example, HATE. Then, opposite—on the other side of the balance—list the person, act, place, and/or event which you feel best is associated with, for example, LOVE.

3. **Mekinges' Last Message**

The story, as you know, begins with a *Prologue—fifteen years* after the "year of the three-legged deer"—when Jesse Benton's son, Takawsu, returns to the place of his birth. His mother, Mekinges (and Jesse's first wife) had died. But suppose she had had time to write down her last thoughts, hopes, and wishes to Jesse, the man she loved, married, and with whom she bore and raised two children. What would these private words have been that Takawsu now brings from his mother?

Name_____

Date_____

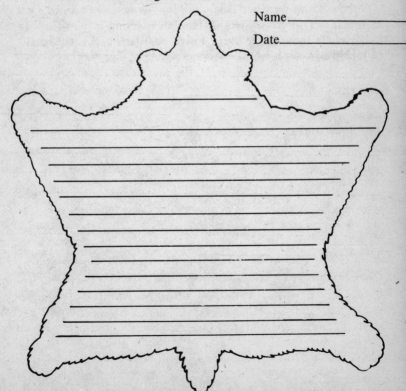

VI. RELATED-TO-READING EXPERIENCES

1. Suppose that President James Monroe had written a letter of commendation to (a) Jesse Benton, (b) Governor James Brown Ray, (c) Skoligiso, or (d) Judge Harvey Sweetz. What would he have said in such a letter? Choose one or more and write a letter for President Monroe.

2. The Delaware and other American Indians made a practice of giving meaningful names to people, animals, the months of the year, and so forth. For example, Takawsu: "he is gentle" or Maskanako: "he is strong." Do some research and try to find out (a) the meaning(s) of your first and/or last name and (b) the reason (if any) for the names of the months in our calendar.

3. In American history, the *frontier* was a continually moving boundary. Try to find out what the part of America described in this story looked like in the early 1800s—where the boundaries were and where the *frontier* actually was. Make a map for future readers of this book, trying in particular to include some of the cities, towns, and landmarks that would help a reader locate the Indiana setting of this story.

WHEN HITLER STOLE PINK RABBIT

Written and Illustrated

by JUDITH KERR

I. THE STORY

Anna was only nine years old in 1933, too busy with her school work and friends to take much notice of Adolf Hitler's face glaring out of political posters all over Berlin. Being Jewish, she thought, was just something you were because your parents and grandparents were Jewish. But then one day her father was unaccountably, frighteningly missing. Soon after, she and her brother, Max, were hurried out of Germany by their mother with alarming secrecy.

Reunited in Switzerland, Anna and her family embark on an adventure that would go on for years, in several different countries. They learn many new things: new languages, how to cope with the wildest confusions, and how to be poor. Anna soon discovers that there are special skills to being a refugee. And as long as the family stayed together, that was all that really mattered.

II. PREREADING DISCUSSION QUESTIONS

The questions which follow are illustrative of the kinds which teachers can prepare for the purpose of releasing children to reveal how they feel *about some of the larger ideas and bigger meanings contained in the book* before it is read by the children.

About Freedom of Expression
   1. It is open house at your school and, along the hall, is your painting for everyone to see! But, much to your

surprise, quite a few of the parents think your picture is *disgraceful! shocking! ugly! dirty! unfit for nice young people to have to look at!* Since some of these parents are very influential, they order the principal to have it taken down, and she obeys. Then they ask to have you suspended from school as a bad influence on the other children. This, too, is done. If you chose not to accept this action, what arguments could you give? What problems would you expect to find once you "won" your battle and were allowed to return to school?

2. What do you think people are referring to when they talk about the *power of the press* (or *radio* or *television*)?

3. Why do you think that so many people who are important businessmen, politicians, or movie and TV stars, for example, seem to be afraid of the press? And, on the other hand, people like you seem to love to see their name in the newspaper?

4. You probably know that there are some newspapers, magazines, and movies that young people *are not allowed* to see. How do you think that this does or does not rob you of some of your freedom?

About Mobility

5. What problems do you think a young person would have, both in and out of school, if your parents had a job where you lived only six or seven months in one place?

6. Suppose that one of your parents was so famous that you had no privacy and you couldn't do the normal, everyday things you enjoy doing because reporters, autograph seekers, the curious, and the silly, question-asking pests are always staring, interfering, and interrupting. What can you list that you think might help as you go from place to place (such as the beach, the movies, a restaurant, or a party) *in secrecy?*

About Thievery

7. How many explanations can you give that could explain what a person is referring to when he/she exclaims: "*I don't care about my money or any of my other possessions, but when you* steal my name *you have robbed me of the only treasure I have!*"

8. What do you think a person might mean when he/she shouts: "*You have robbed me of five years of my life!*"?

9. What do you think a person of about twenty-five years of age could mean when he/she says: "*My childhood was stolen from me!*"?

III. PREREADING ACTIVITIES

The Prereading Activities which follow purpose to elicit *analogous* or *parallel* experiences from the reader's background so that he/she can identify more intensely with the *feelings* of the characters in the book—as they interact with other characters, situations, and events—as he/she reads and finds them familiar because they are but one step removed from the real occurrences in his/her life.

1. Pack for Your Life

Suddenly something strange, urgent, and mysterious happens in your family: Your parents tell you that you've just *one* day to pack *a small suitcase* with those personal and valuable things you own (except for clothes which they will pack in a trunk for you). They only tell you that the chances are very slim that you will ever return again and that everything else that won't fit into the one suitcase must be considered lost forever. In the "suitcase" below, pack those things which you would take with you under these circumstances. Think about everything you have—the toys, games, keepsakes, souvenirs, and so forth. On the number corresponding to the one in the "suitcase," name or describe the article. You can use only *one* numeral for *one* article! Thus, if you have two blocks or two pieces of jewelry, for example, you will need to use *two* spaces in the suitcase. Think carefully! Be selective! Then . . . pack for your life!

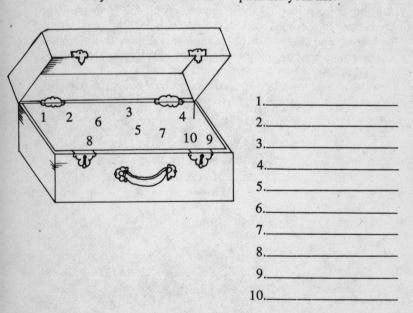

1._____
2._____
3._____
4._____
5._____
6._____
7._____
8._____
9._____
10._____

IV. POSTREADING DISCUSSION QUESTIONS

1. What problems would you expect Anna and Max to have once they are settled in England?

2. Anna and her family get on the wrong train—a train going *to Germany* (p. 94–95). How might their lives have been changed had they stayed on that train?

3. On page 67, Anna says: *"I think I might quite like being a refugee."* How do you think she might have felt about being a refugee by the time the family reached England?

4. Although the title of this book is *When Hitler Stole Pink Rabbit,* Pink Rabbit is hardly ever mentioned (reread pages 27 and 47) and seems to have little to do with the story. And even Anna laughs at her own incredulous thought that Hitler would "snuggle" her Pink Rabbit. Now that you've finished the story and can think back on it as a whole, what possible reasons can you give that would explain why you think the author chose this particular title for the story?

5. Why do you think that Anna and Max were so *naïve* about Hitler and the Nazis and about being Jews?

6. Of the many incidents of prejudice which occur in this story, which would you choose to explain as the one which made you feel the most uncomfortable and sad?

7. If one assumes that Onkel Julius *isn't* stupid, how then can you explain that he chose to remain in Germany?

8. What do you think was the hardest adjustment Anna, Max, Mama, and Papa *each* had to make as a result of suddenly being poor?

V. HELPING CHILDREN TO REVEAL THEIR COMPREHENSION

1. Significant Symbols

DIRECTIONS: As you now know, Adolf Hitler didn't actually steal Anna's Pink Rabbit; yet, Pink Rabbit is symbolic of Anna—and almost all children during Hitler's reign (especially German Jews)—of the things she lost, compromises she had to make, difficult changes she had to endure, and so forth. Pictured below are five additional symbols of significance to this particular story. On the lines near each, think of as many "connections" as you can and how each is symbolic of the changes in the lives and living of Papa, Mama, Max, and Anna.

The
Schooling of
Anna and Max

_____

_____

_____

_____

_____

_____

Omama and Pumpel

_____

_____

_____

_____

_____

_____

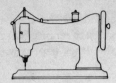

Mama, Madame Fernand, and the Sewing Machine Incident

_____
_____
_____
_____
_____
_____
_____
_____

Onkel Julius
and His
Old Silver
Watch

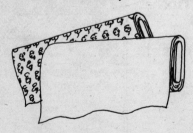

_____
_____
_____
_____
_____
_____
_____
_____

Great-Aunt Sarah's
Cloth for the "Needy"

_____
_____
_____
_____
_____
_____
_____
_____
_____

2. Front-Page News Scoop!

Anna and her family have just stepped off the train in London, and you, *The London News'* star reporter, happened to be on hand to scoop all the other papers with this escape odyssey!

"All the Views that make The News!"

The London News

Vol._____ No._____   September 27, 1935   Price_____

FAMOUS NEWSMAN TO TURN TALENTS TO TELEVISION SCRIPT ON NAPOLEON

by_____

(London News Tele-foto)

HITLER WINS 'ELECTION'

"I think I might quite like being a refugee"

—o—

TEN-YEAR-OLD GIRL TELLS OF ESCAPE FROM NAZI GERMANY

by_____

3. **Signs of the Times**

DIRECTIONS: One of the popular ways today to let people know what you approve or disapprove of is to make a sign to "protest" for or against people, things, or ideas. Probably all the major characters in this story would carry a protest sign against Hitler, but what other people, things, or ideas would each of them design and carry? You be the signmaker for them!

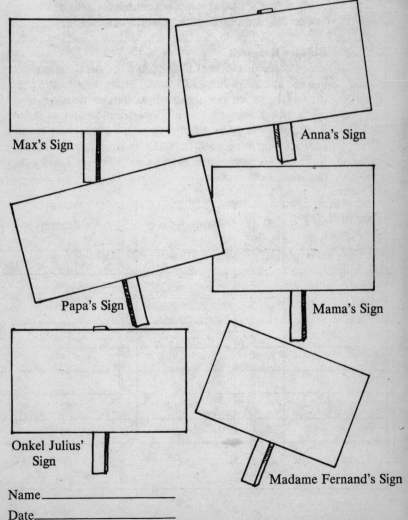

Max's Sign

Anna's Sign

Papa's Sign

Mama's Sign

Onkel Julius' Sign

Madame Fernand's Sign

Name_____

Date_____

VI. RELATED-TO-READING EXPERIENCES

1. **Geographic Forms of Address**

   Anna and her parents and brother travel from Germany to Switzerland, to France, and to England. In each locale, we find people being addressed in different ways (Herr So-and-So or Madame What's-Her-Name). In our country, we use Mr., Mrs., Miss, and Ms. What equivalents can you find for these in other countries? Collect as many as you can and put them on a world map.

2. **Refugee Research**

   People of different nationalities, political beliefs, religions, and races have had to flee from their birthplaces for widely varied reasons, such as natural disaster, war, religious beliefs, "a better life," persecution and so forth. Turn back the pages of history and, on the chart below (or one you may wish to make yourself), record your Refugee Research data. Some easy starters: Lutherans, the Irish, Armenians.

Type of Refugee Group	Date	From - To	Reason

MS READ-a-thon — a simple way to start youngsters reading

Boys and girls between 6 and 14 can join the MS READ-a-thon and help find a cure for Multiple Sclerosis by reading books. And they get two rewards — the enjoyment of reading, and the great feeling that comes from helping others.

Parents and educators: For complete information call your local MS chapter. Or mail the coupon below.

Kids can help, too!

ABOUT THE AUTHOR

Charles F. Reasoner is one of America's most popular and energetic promoters of juvenile literature. Much sought after for his popular seminars, lectures, and workshops in the teaching of reading and children's literature, he has taught every grade from kindergarten through sixth. He is Professor of Children's Literature at New York University, and has been a consultant for Yearling Books since its inception in 1966.